Published by Semiotext(e)
PO BOX 629, South Pasadena, CA 91031
www.semiotexte.com

Cover: David Wojnarowicz, *Untitled*, 1988. Acrylic on two chromogenic contact sheets, mounted on glass 11 x 13 ¼ inches. Courtesy of the Estate of David Wojnarowicz and P·P·O·W, New York.

Design: Hedi El Kholti
ISBN: 978-1-63590-128-3

Distributed by the MIT Press, Cambridge, MA, and London, England.
Printed and bound in the United States of America.

10 9 8 7 6 5 4 3 2

THE FREEZER DOOR

Mattilda Bernstein Sycamore

semiotext(e)

To everyone who still dreams of the city
To everyone who still dreams in the city
To everyone who still dreams

For JoAnne, 1974–1995
For Chrissie Contagious, 1974–2010
For David Wojnarowicz, 1954–1992

One problem with gentrification is that it always gets worse.

But then I go into a Hooters, and it's a vintage clothing store. A friend of mine is trying on breasts. This is why I like dreaming.

I remember when faggots kissed hello. We had so much to fear and so we feared nothing, I mean we feared one another but we feared fear more. Kissing one another on the lips, this was joyous and commonplace, a legacy we were inheriting, an art—how to stretch out our lips in front of our faces, how to queen it up in front of a loving or hostile public, how to emphasize connection or disdain.

We kissed hello because we had to. We had to know we could kiss like this, a simple greeting but something splendid and transgressive even when mundane, or that's what it felt like for me when I moved to San Francisco in 1992, and I was 19. This kiss didn't necessarily feel like a radical act, it was just something you did if you were a faggot, whether in suit and tie or broadcasting the pageantry of outsider imagination. Was this something that united us? I wouldn't have said so then, but maybe I'm saying it now.

Yes, there were the ones who turned their cheeks, too good for this kiss unless they explained the sudden turn by mentioning a cold sore, one just starting or one in the past, whichever way we hoped we were taking care. Sometimes you knew someone had really bad breath, but you kissed her on the lips anyway, it was okay to endure a little discomfort to avoid seeming snotty or scared. Unless this was one of those queens who would grab you and start feeling you up, that was a good reason to avoid contact.

You kissed the ones you loved and the ones you didn't even like that much, sometimes even someone you hated, just so you wouldn't seem shady. Too much garlic was never a problem, we kissed anyway. We kissed the living and the dying, knowing that the dying were part of the living and we wanted to keep them with us.

Maybe this was a dream—I mean I know it wasn't a dream then, but maybe it is now. Now we're more afraid, afraid of one another, so even the gestures of intimacy disappear. Most of the time I don't even think of kissing someone hello anymore, I reach for a hug if possible and this can be beautiful too, but in a different way. How strange to think that in the early-'90s, when it felt like everyone was dying, we were less fearful in certain ways.

When I'm washing my hair in the shower, and suddenly I think what the hell am I doing? Oh, I'm in the shower—this is one of the things I do in the shower. Sometimes repetition leads to revelation, and sometimes revelation leads to repetition, which leads to no revelation ever again.

You know when you notice someone's looking at you, but you're not sure, so you do the same thing you were just doing, so you don't look like you're looking? I was holding a piece of chewed-up licorice root in front of my face in between two fingers, getting ready to throw it out the window. He lit a cigarette. I hate cigarettes, but that's the place for them, downstairs and outside and away from my window. He crossed the street, looked back, waited, so then I literally leaned out the window. He came back. Eventually I said do you want to come up? And he did. That's when I knew my life could start again.

There's a certain kind of knowledge, growing up in a particular body, socialized to be a particular thing you will never be, knowing this and learning to grow with it instead of against. Maybe I'm saying we all need different kinds of people in our lives, right? When anything becomes homogenous, there's a problem. When anything becomes so homogenous that people don't even think about it, that's worse.

I used to live in a neighborhood where no one belonged, and so we all belonged. Now I live in a neighborhood where faggots look at me like I don't belong, and so I don't. Soon they won't belong either, but this won't make anything better.

There's too much desire without desire. Too much desire for desire. Not enough desire. Sometimes we remember the dead, and forget the living dead. And sometimes we forget everything. We make art so we don't die. And still we die. Silence is a kind of memory, but memory should never be a form of silencing. Maybe there are exceptions. I know a process can be collective, and a collective can be in-process, but what about a collective process without collective process?

Knowing the gap between what you want and what you yearn for, can there be hope in this? Maybe I'm saying that yearning often comes from spurning, the brokenness from that glance, the desire for seamlessness. Maybe there's no way not to be broken, only a way not to feel broken.

But then I actually make the move, first my leg close to his, then my hand a friendly brush against his cheek, eventually we're making out and this is when my brain can relax. Maybe not just my brain but everything. This is what it means to have a body.

The conversation is important because it's not important. This is what people do at bars.

At some point he asks me where I live. His name's Caleb. I ask him if he wants to come home with me. He says: I'm undetectable.

Where's the transition, I mean it's like he's online. I guess some people are always online.

I say I'm negative. He asks me if I fuck raw, he says he wants to fuck my brains out. I say no, I use condoms—but we don't have to fuck, there are lots of other things we can do.

The truth is that I wasn't even thinking about fucking, I just wanted to continue the way this was making me feel. He says no it's not going to work out.

But still I'm here, in my body. I want to be here. I want to be here, in my body. With him. You're adorable, he says, later, when he's back and we're making out again.

Adorable—I love that word.

He asks me where I live again. I guess he's that drunk.

He yells over at some guy who just arrived: *I wanna fuck the shit out of you.*

I remember a phone sex ad from 2001, with someone who looked just like this other guy, pretending to be a gas station attendant with rhinestone studs in his ears and jeans with textured pockets. We can't always be attracted to people we don't immediately think are tragic. The way my heart stops a little and I feel the sensation of not moving. But why? I don't want anyone to fuck my brains out.

Caleb says let's switch positions, so now I'm next to James, who makes clothes. He likes my clothes. Maybe Caleb wants me to go home with James, is this strange or kind or a little bit of both I'm not sure but I like James too.

This is what happens at bars, or can happen, if you're lucky.

James says do you live in Seattle? Because I've never seen you around. And I say that's because I don't go out. So he wants to know why.

Somehow I feel so comfortable, even though I'm wondering what this comfort means, how I could feel comfortable in this world where I don't exist anymore, a world I've fled, a world that rarely welcomes me, a world I need so fucking badly or maybe I'm not thinking all of this yet. I say I don't go out because of the smoke, even smoke machines—because I don't drink—and because I deal with a lot of chronic health problems.

I'm worried about being too serious, here at this table with these fags I've just met, you're not supposed to be too serious at bars.

But how do Caleb and I end up in the bathroom together, I guess it's after he shows me a picture of his dick on his phone, I mean he says it's an accident but I'll take foreplay any way I can get it so we're making out against the wall by the toilet and then he's pushing me downward so I'm on my knees, yes, his dick in my mouth, someone comes in and maybe Caleb's ready to pull away, but I could stay here all night. Then we're in the bathroom that locks, he smacks my face kind of hard and I love it—how could this sex already feel so connected, now he's sucking my cock, pulling on my nipples, but then I say that's too hard, rub my chest, and then he does it right.

I ask him if he wants me to smack his face too, he doesn't, somehow this is kind of funny and then he stands up and says that was your chance.

My chance for what?

Your chance to get off.

I didn't know I was trying to get off.

Later, he's telling me I'm adorable again, I really do love that word. He leaves to go home, but then he's back, and he looks really sad.

I start to say did you just have a mood swing, but I stop myself because maybe that's too familiar. What happened, I say, and he says it's nothing, I just missed the bus.

I say I just got really sad because you're sad, is that okay?

Are we making out, or just petting each other, or am I just petting him—he's adorable, is that okay to say, even while he's sad? Do you see how I'm so present? How this presence can mean so much, even in a situation that really means nothing.

He doesn't want my number, I already know that. He has a boyfriend. Everyone in the bar is smashed because this is Sunday night, Sunday night early but early Sunday night is the messiest. This is why people are hooking up in the bathroom, this is why people are being honest, at least some of the people, but I like it even if it's the messiness that makes people more open—I don't need it but maybe they do. Beneath the shade and the shame and the sadness, there's a sweetness, and I haven't felt this in years I mean have I ever.

So I'm walking home with James, I mean he's walking to the next bar and I'm walking him there on my way home. Everyone was exchanging stories at the bar, so I ask him if it's okay to talk about Caleb, does Caleb always get sad like that, is he a sad drunk?

We talk about what we do, whatever that means but there's a connection I think, I mean I need to come back into the world, maybe even this world. I kiss James goodbye, I mean we kiss goodbye, and I make it into the kiss that means we're making out until he indicates with his hands that that's enough and then we say we'll get together soon. This is a part of me that I want to be part of, I mean I want this back. How long it's been since I've had fag friends in my daily life. How much longer it's been since I've dated anyone I mean over a decade. What my body needs in order to be a body that's not just a body of needs. I'm getting really emotional. I'm right at the edge of being able to cry.

When I get home, the phone is ringing and I see that it's James, he's calling to give me his number because he forgot that he already gave me his number. I feel like I'm back in my body and I'm shut down. I'm so close to crying. Somewhere there's a place in my body where I can actually feel alive.

Walking through Tashkent in the morning and doesn't that sound romantic, but really it's just the name of a tiny park of dirt and dogshit—someone comes rushing up to me and says I hope this doesn't sound weird, but I saw you on the bus the other day, and I really like the way you dress. He looks like the awkward best friend from one of those movies in the '80s except he was probably born in the '90s—in a month he's flying to Bangkok to travel through Southeast Asia because he doesn't know what he's doing with his life. I wonder what Bangkok means for him—is he a white kid in search of adventure or a mixed-race kid in search of something deeper, I'm already three blocks away but this is what I'm thinking about.

And then, as I'm getting closer to the real park, Volunteer, I mean I like everything about this park except its name in honor of the volunteers in the Spanish-American War, the way colonialism is always there, even when we're looking at the trees and just as I'm about to enter the park I hear someone saying hell-lo! I look over, and there's an older woman with curly gray hair in a sleek silver car, slowing down to stop the car behind her, and I figure she's going to ask for directions, but instead she says YOU. LOOK. FABULOUS.

And then I get a rush through my body, this is what I'm looking for, this feeling of feeling what's going on inside, me, and then at the end of the walk, when I'm getting closer to home, tired now, looking in at the yoga boutique to see a black tank top with shiny copper lettering that says, wait, already I can't remember, one of those yoga slogans, fill in the blank, next to tie-dye print hotpants, and a blue sweatshirt reading LOVE IS ALL YOU NEED, because really all you need is this sweatshirt.

When you wonder what you've always wondered but in a different way, maybe this is what it means to grow. To move into a new space of wondering.

I want my body to feel my body. I want my body to feel.

Sometimes I feel invisible, which is not the same thing as saying I am invisible. I'm leaving Volunteer Park again, at the end of another morning walk. Some guy's following me in his car, but I'm kind of in denial about it because it's the middle of the day, so you can't miss all my earrings, or the long red women's coat that fits like a dress. And, because I'm wearing a purple hat with a flower on it—faggots are so afraid of flowers. Probably he's straight.

I have a private garage, he says, before driving me into a building where every parking spot is taken. I need to piss. He opens the door to a stairwell—you can piss here, no one ever uses this stairwell. What do you like to do, he says, and I don't have the answer because I'm attracted to the dynamic, but not to him. First of all, way too much cologne.

He wants to fuck me, which sounds pretty hot in this stairwell with the unfinished stairs and cement floor, but he doesn't have a condom. We can go next door, he says, RiteAid, which isn't next door.

I say we can go to my place, and when we get inside he starts to sit on my bed and I say don't sit there, I'm pretty sensitive to cologne, I hope that's okay. Of course he has poppers, even though he says he wasn't looking for sex. He fucks me on the floor in the entryway, maybe not the best thing for my knees. When he's done, he throws the condom in the toilet. Luckily he doesn't flush. He says are you shy, you seem pretty shy.

But I might have just been invited to a covert Super Bowl party. I keep listening to Mark's message to see if it says we will be watching football, or we won't. There's something about making vegan curry, but do you think it's a trap? What if I get there, and everyone's wearing Seahawks helmets and cock-socks?

Suddenly it's very quiet. I guess I should go outside while the game is going on, and then get back home before it ends, right? Sudden memories of my father screaming at the TV. He thought that if he screamed loud enough, this would make him working-class—just one of the guys, getting drunk in front of the TV. A working-class psychiatrist.

I don't know which is worse, people who watch football because they like football, or people who watch because everyone else is watching.

Now I'm in another gay bar. I knew it would be awful, but I didn't know it would be this awful.

When someone asks WHAT'S YOUR REAL NAME, you might be in the wrong place. When four different people ask WHAT'S YOUR REAL NAME, you're definitely in the wrong place.

Then there's the queen who says are you a boy or a girl—JUST KIDDING!!! People at gay bars have really evolved.

This queen was dating someone who had my haircut, he was 25 and she thought he really liked her, but then he said she was too feminine. And short.

I am short, she says.

She doesn't like it when people say how old are you, what a ridiculous question. Then she says: How old are you?

She had sex with one of the barbacks, but she didn't like it when he said he usually likes to fuck several guys in a row. They were at a bathhouse.

Every gay bar is an accidental comedy routine. The best comedy routine is the one that takes itself seriously.

When you see a sign in the bathroom that says ANYONE CAUGHT SELLING OR USING DRUGS WILL BE BANNED FROM THIS ESTABLISHMENT, you know where to find drugs.

When someone in the bathroom says I've never been pee-shy before in my entire life—is this a compliment? I end up watching the guys playing pool in the room that isn't so overheated, drunken hipsters humping the table, kind of out of place in this bar where the suburban imagination hasn't even caught on to hipsterism. The hottest one for me is kind of butch but he's wearing this T-shirt with little flowers on it—I'm in love with that T-shirt, I mean I'm in love with that T-shirt on him. He comes over to introduce himself and when I hold out my hand he does that thing like he's confused that I'm not offering a proper masculine handshake, but somehow I don't mind because I like the feeling of his hand so much. He keeps looking at me, and later he says he's going outside to smoke but he'll be back, so I lean over to kiss him, just to be friendly but also to see what might happen and what happens is that he turns away and reaches for my hand again. But I don't need another handshake so I kiss his neck—what matters is that I've gone up to the one I'm most attracted to, I've gone up and I've made a move and now it's time for me to go home.

Suddenly remembering all those times when I reached my hand out for someone to crush me. Without the trauma of mandatory masculinity, what would I be? I still remember that cactus I threw out the window as a kid when it poked me, and then it just grew and grew. When I say hi, my name's Mattilda, and then everything's over. It doesn't matter how hot he thought I was before, he will never think that way again. What would it be like without this damage, over and over again? I can't remember the last time someone asked what I would do if I was stuck on a desert island.

Before I threw the cactus out the window, I found a worm on the sidewalk, and I was playing with it, pressing a stick into its squishy body to see which way it would move—I pressed a little harder, and it split in half. So then there were two worms. Was this possible? They were still moving around. Until I realized that worm was dead. I had killed it. I didn't want to kill anything ever again. I watched the ants building their cities, wondering what I looked like to them.

This city that is and isn't a city, but I guess that's what every city is becoming now, a destination to imagine what imagination might be like, except for the lack. Some terrible things are worse than other terrible things, but this doesn't mean we need more terrible things.

Sometimes going to the grocery store makes me feel less alone. Sometimes I'm trying to tell someone about this new opening in my life, and I end up feeling closed. When I say opening, I mean the possibility that when I feel I won't feel like I shouldn't feel. My body in a room with other bodies feeling me feeling my body. When I say this room I mean you. When I say you I mean make room.

On a good day, I write in sentences. On a bad day, I write in thoughts. You know when you're dreaming, and past and present blend together in a way that makes it feel like maybe you can imagine a future? And then you wake up. Dreaming is not quite escape, not quite thinking, not quite feeling, or is it? Because sometimes I feel so much more hopeful when I'm asleep, like this is the day when everything changes, I mean once I wake up, or maybe I'm already awake, but not quite, because it's that possibility of living in two times or experiences at once, but in the same body, the one that lets me down as soon as I get out of bed.

Every time I shave, I get the same shaving cut. It's like it's lying there dormant, waiting for the blade. I don't understand when I chop my finger instead of the onion. I don't understand why nothing heals.

I'm kind of new to this, says the ice cube. Don't ever leave me, says the ice cube tray.

I'm melting, says the ice cube. Why can't it always be this way, says the ice cube tray.

Everyone likes me when I'm cold, says the ice cube tray. But I want to be fluid, says the ice cube. Hold me.

I'm always holding you, says the ice cube tray. Then I want to live on my own, says the ice cube. No one appreciates me, says the ice cube tray.

Explain gentrification to me, says the ice cube. Crushed ice, says the ice cube tray.

What about global warming, asks the ice cube. Even I'm going to melt, says the ice cube tray. Let's watch Olympic figure skating.

Stop, you're giving me nightmares, says the ice cube.

Cocktails, says the ice cube tray. You're mean, says the ice cube. Okay: icemaker. Slush, says the ice cube tray. Recycling, says the ice cube. Snow cone, says the ice cube tray. Okay, I'm sick of arguing, says the ice cube. We need a mediator.

Can you believe some people put ice in their coffee, says the ice cube tray? I don't even want to talk about it, says the ice cube. But sometimes I wish you wouldn't squeeze me so tightly.

Okay, I'll try to loosen up, says the ice cube tray. But I can't promise you won't slip away. Let's not think about that, says the ice cube. Is there anyone else around? Just us, says the ice cube tray. I like it best this way.

Tell me you love me, says the ice cube. I like you a lot, says the ice cube tray.

Tell me you'll never leave me, says the ice cube. I can't say that, says the ice cube tray. What is love, anyway?

If I'm not free to leave, is this really an open relationship, asks the ice cube. The only open relationship is the open door, says the ice cube tray.

Are you trying to scare me with a metaphor, asks the ice cube.

Let's watch videos of the North Pole, says the ice cube tray. No, the South Pole, says the ice cube.

But there are people at the South Pole, says the ice cube tray. Good point, says the ice cube. Are there penguins at the North Pole?

I liked that movie about penguins, says the ice cube tray. Me too, says the ice cube, but can we watch it on mute this time? I didn't like that voiceover. Or the classical music. I just want to hear the penguins.

What do you think about satire, asks the ice cube? I don't understand it, says the ice cube tray.

People talk about freezing temperatures like that's a bad thing, says the ice cube. Where would we be without freezing temperatures, asks the ice cube tray.

Why are there so many songs about holding on, says the ice cube. People don't understand pain, says the ice cube tray.

Have you ever felt hopeful, asks the ice cube tray. I don't understand hope, says the ice cube.

Maybe it's like when the lights go off, says the ice cube tray.

Sing me a happy song, says the ice cube. "You're as cold as ice, you're as cold as ice, you're as cold as ice, I kno-ow," sings the ice cube tray.

Nobody is innocent, says the ice cube. You're not as experienced as you think you are, says the ice cube tray. Experience isn't everything, says the ice cube. What else is there, says the ice cube tray. Feeling, says the ice cube. I don't understand, says the ice cube tray.

Do you believe in God, asks the ice cube. How could I, says the ice cube tray.

What does it mean when someone says a relationship is on ice, asks the ice cube. It means you love me, says the ice cube tray.

"Ice Ice Baby" is one of my favorite songs, says the ice cube. It's underrated, says the ice cube tray. But Ice Cube is a better rapper. Flattery will get you anywhere, says the ice cube. Although I don't know if I really understand pop culture. We're not the intended audience, says the ice cube tray.

People talk about the Ice Age like we're not part of this world, says the ice cube.

Are we, asks the ice cube tray.

Why do people hate poetry, asks the ice cube. Because it's like us, says the ice cube tray.

I don't know if we're getting anywhere, says the ice cube. An honest acknowledgment of the situation is a first step, says the ice cube tray.

Sometimes I wonder if there's anything else out there, says the ice cube. We all do, says the ice cube tray.

What do you do when you're not in the freezer, asks the ice cube. You don't want to know, says the ice cube tray.

I wish you wouldn't be so evasive, says the ice cube. It's for your own benefit, says the ice cube tray.

Do ice cubes go to heaven, asks the ice cube. Only people believe in heaven, says the ice cube tray.

Let's cuddle, says the ice cube. I love cuddling, says the ice cube tray.

Sometimes I feel like I'm lost, says the ice cube. We're all lost, says the ice cube tray.

I still don't understand what it means to save up for a rainy day, says the ice cube. It means always use an umbrella, says the ice cube tray.

Explain violence to me, says the ice cube. Someone turns off the electricity, says the ice cube tray.

What is the meaning of life, asks the ice cube. There's no future for us, says the ice cube tray. But sometimes I like living in denial.

Explain nihilism to me, says the ice cube. Everything melts, says the ice cube tray.

Explain existentialism, says the ice cube. This isn't freedom, says the ice cube tray.

Explain democracy, says the ice cube. This is democracy, says the ice cube tray.

Explain communism, says the ice cube. We're in this together, says the ice cube tray.

Explain anarchism, says the ice cube. No one understands anarchism, says the ice cube tray.

I don't understand people, says the ice cube. Even people don't understand people, says the ice cube tray.

What is it like to gamble, asks the ice cube. Open the freezer door, says the ice cube tray.

When you turn the music off, and suddenly you feel an unbearable sadness, that means turn the music back on, right? When you still feel the sadness, even with the music, that means there's something wrong with this music. Sometimes I feel like sex without context isn't sex at all. And sometimes I feel like sex without context is what sex should always be.

When you write something broken, is it important to feel broken? When you write something unbroken, is it important? Even just sitting next to someone who casually puts his hand on my leg, this means so much to me. Yes, he has a boyfriend who's sitting right next to us, and this is okay too. What I'm saying is that I want my body back, my whole body, my whole experience of the world.

I've spent so much time trying to find the places and spaces where I can interact without feeling broken, but this hasn't worked. I can no longer live in queer worlds where I am intellectually and emotionally present, but I don't have an embodied self.

Sometimes, when you don't write about something, it goes away. And sometimes, when you don't write about something, it never goes away. This guy on the radio says he writes in a sense of elation in the morning. A sense of elation. For several hours every day, very early. Maybe I misheard him? He said getting directions but I thought he said getting erections.

When I was a kid, I made up happy lyrics for sad songs. This is called denial. One thing about language is that sometimes it hurts. Or, it doesn't hurt, and then you do.

Acknowledging inconsistency doesn't have to mean embracing it. Or shouldn't, I don't think, but most people don't seem to realize this. The desire to sound reasonable, when the only way to say something meaningful is to sound unreasonable.

My mother says that whenever she doesn't hear back from me for a few days, she feels like that time when I went missing for 24 or 48 hours, and then I appeared in the driveway and she took me to Suburban Hospital to see if I'd had a concussion. I don't remember this at all—I do remember that every weekend in high school, I would leave after screaming fights with my father, who didn't want to pay for a cab or books or a restaurant or whatever it was that I wanted, he just wanted to scream. I would leave for as long as I could. But my mother doesn't remember my father screaming at me—she remembers my father screaming at her.

By the end of high school, I stayed at my father's office every weekend, even when I didn't have anything to do—it was a studio apartment where he'd added a wall to create a waiting room for his patients, with copies of *Time* and *New York Magazine* instead of the *New Yorker* like the other psychiatrists. I'd always wanted to live in an apartment—when I stayed at my father's office I could almost pretend I had my own place, with a bathroom in two parts and the tiniest kitchen. I would study the way my father's pens were arranged, and the exact placement of every tissue box, but my friends weren't as careful—it wasn't as easy to conceal a cigarette burn in the carpet as it was to move the tissue box back, so that's when my father found out. But then I said do you really want me driving home drunk? That was my argument, the argument that worked. I needed to beat my father on his terms, because those were the only terms.

When someone at a bar compliments my outfit, and then says he used to be more daring, but then he got older, I'm guessing he thinks I'm a lot younger than he is. But then he says he went home for the holidays, and found this Nine Inch Nails T-shirt from when he was in sixth grade, and he must've worn it for gym class because it still really smelled, and if he was in sixth grade when he had a Nine Inch Nails T-shirt, that means he's at least four years younger than me.

Some markers of young adulthood are dated, and some are fated. So I try to get to the bottled water scene in *Heathers*, but it's too scary when Christian Slater shoots one of the jocks and then the other one starts running shirtless through the woods. I don't like homophobia, even when it's supposed to be a critique of homophobia. The tyranny of masculinity must end. Also, the masculinity of tyranny. And, tyranny.

I watched *Heathers* in high school, but continued to drink bottled water. Was this an act of resistance? It turns out the joke is about mineral water—they plant it with a suicide note so it looks like the guys were gay. Along with rouge and porn and Valentine's candy and a photo of Judy Garland.

But how would high school kids in 1988 or '89 understand Judy Garland as a symbol of homosexual bonding? I'm still not sure that I do. Before I spent the weekends at my father's office, I would meet him there after school, so he could drive me home. I would wait upstairs in the library next to the rooftop pool. In the library where I would jerk off to the dream of New York in *Interview* magazine, come all over the pages, then I had to find more pages. Until I discovered the cruising bathrooms down the street and then I would go there almost every day—I didn't call it sex because there was no way I wouldn't deserve to die, if I didn't feel it then maybe I would win.

All these guys older than my father, craving what was between my legs, but did anyone ever speak? Maybe a note on toilet paper, toilet paper wrapped around a pen, and passed underneath the bathroom stall. But no one ever said do you need help or hope or a hug or somewhere to hide or information, a way out or a way in, a key, an escape route, a path beyond brokenness, a field of sunflowers, a record-breaking snowstorm, nourishment, an end to the nightmares, a new way of living, a gap in the sky, a break from desperation, a future beyond hollowness, some new music to listen to on your Walkman in bed.

I don't remember the first time I saw the pen but I do remember the clenching in my chest, the nervousness before unlocking the stall and following the route of the guy who'd written the note. Eventually I was the one to pass the pen first, leading guys into the stairwell, and all the way to the bottom of the parking garage where the stairwell ended and we almost had our own room.

Once, I brought someone to my father's office—I didn't know how cute he was until he followed me and my note all the way down the stairwell but then he said do you live around here? He wasn't that much older than me, but he was old enough to think I was old enough to live alone. My father wasn't in his office, so after a silent walk that felt like days we were naked on that analytic couch, naked together, it was over too fast. And then he was the one who looked away.

I remember one guy who insisted on driving me home, so I let him drive me the three blocks to my father's office— or to the lobby, anyway. Speaking of lobbies, he gave me his card—he was a lobbyist, that's what it said. He told me to call any time, but I didn't know what that would mean. Was he risking it all for the fever of underage cock, or did he want to offer me something I may never find?

I'm reading another book of nostalgia for New York in the 1970s—Rose Kennedy walks into the bookstore, and asks you to choose the photos for her memoir. This will never happen again. But uncritical consumption of critical engagement is still uncritical engagement. The problem with true confessions is there aren't any, but it's amazing how many ugly 1960s buildings have beautiful wood floors. Sometimes you slip and say something you don't mean to say, and this is the best and worst moment.

My mother calls to tell me about a play where a straight guy invites a gay guy into his bed after he's been assaulted, because the gay guy can no longer sleep alone, and I'm thinking of course the straight guy is the hero, but then my mother says: It was one of the most beautiful things I've seen in a while. A while, she says again, and I'm crying, quietly, so she doesn't know, and afterwards she says what did you think of my description of the play?

The weirdest thing about a sunny day in Seattle is that you think it will happen again. I love watching people stop to watch the sunset. I love watching people. I love watching the sunset. I'm walking by an elementary school playground, and this kid looks up at me, and says: Do you want to help me shut down a McDonald's?

But I'm living in a city that's suddenly obsessed with football—it's like high school all over again, except my high school didn't even have football. Watching these guys hump each other at a gay bar because the Seahawks won, I'm grossed out at the cause but still somehow grateful that at least they're expressing desire in a celebratory way until the humping gives way to chants of U-S-A and I'm chilled by how quickly excessive masculinity escalates into patriotism meaning war.

Remembering when I met Tara-Michelle Ziniuk, and she said: "You called it feminism, and I called it anarchism, and it's the same thing." And she was right.

I remember the playground, where they called me sissy and faggot before I knew what those words meant, but I knew they meant I would never belong. I remember when my father called my mother stupid, over and over and over, for asking him questions about the subject he knew the most about, while she was studying for a graduate degree. I remember deciding to do my own dishes, because I didn't think my mother should do everyone's, and deciding to clean my own room, because I thought it was unjust that my parents hired someone to do this for them. I remember watching my female-socialized friends developing crushes on all the boys we used to hate together, the boys that still hated me.

I didn't know about feminism when I was four on that playground, or eight and listening to my father control everyone in the house with his masculine rage, or 12 and deciding to do my own dishes, or 13 and witnessing the violence of teenage courtship. And the first time I stepped into a feminist space, the conversation was about whether men could identify as feminists—I knew I would never be a man, but I also knew this question was about me.

Somehow I also knew at 18 that feminism was a politic and not a particular type of body, and that it was a politic that would hold me, would hold me together, that I would hold, that would help me to be bold, that would allow me to develop the analysis I needed to survive.

Sometimes there are so many dreams in one night that it's hard to imagine how they all fit. Sometimes there are so many nightmares that it's hard to remember to dream.

Sometimes there's so much dust under the bed that you have another bed there. Remembering when I was 14, and cruising public bathrooms, and I would stare at the automatic air fresheners in the walls to see if they were cameras. When someone asks how you're feeling, and you tell them, and then they want to tell you why you're feeling the way you're feeling, you wonder why they asked.

Lying in bed thinking I hear someone screaming, is someone screaming? Wait, that's my breath.

Without feminism there would be no queer, but without queer there would be no feminism, at least not for queers like me. And yet why do I now feel disembodied in oppositional queer spaces? It's something about the bodies that aren't welcome, including mine. Loyalty to scene masquerading as critical engagement—somehow this never fails to demoralize me. The hierarchies are different, yes, but they're still hierarchies.

I walk around my neighborhood, and there are fags everywhere, but none of these fags intersect with the queer worlds that once meant everything to me. Gay male culture has always sheltered the worst kinds of violence—racism, classism, misogyny, body fascism, self-hatred—so that's why I chose queer worlds instead. And maybe at first it made sense that the bodies like mine were rarely in queer spaces—we had to prove we weren't the enemy. But if I, as someone who has formed oppositional queer spaces and been formed by them over the last two-and-a-half decades, now feel a sense of bodily unease when I'm present, how could other faggots without a history of political instigation and queer analysis ever feel welcome? And, if this is never the case, how will they ever learn the tools to become something other than the wreckage of consumerist craving?

When I moved to Seattle in 2012, people reached out because they knew my work, or they knew people who knew my work, so they knew me. These were queer women and people on the transmasculine spectrum. And I asked for suggestions of fags I might want to date, or at least fags I could talk to about dating. And everyone I met could only come up with two names. That's how dramatic gender segregation is in the queer worlds allegedly dedicated to annihilating borders. No one even thinks about it, because the rhetoric is about self-determination, but whose selves are being determined?

I've always been a part of feminism, and I've always been apart. Apart from the feminism that is only or almost only about women, which, if we must be honest, is most feminism. I don't just mean the types of feminism that embrace blatantly exclusionary practices. Even the intersectional feminist worlds that infuse my analysis are relatively comfortable thinking almost exclusively about women. Which women is the question, and the framework has finally broadened to include trans women. But I rarely see more than a handful of trans women in politicized queer spaces, and male-socialized fags and other transfeminine queers are also absent.

I used to believe that desire formed me, and maybe it did, but if only the bodies that are desired are welcome, then desire is a dead-end. We speak in the languages we were taught to speak, in order to undo the languages we were taught to speak. I dreamed that my headache was gone. But then I woke up. Suddenly I'm wondering about the person who invented the phrase "The coast is clear." Did they live on the coast?

The best thing about reading is when there's no need for an endpoint. And, the best reading is the desire to get to the end. The end of the need or the need for the end?

Someone just stopped me on the street to tell me I look exactly like Boy George. This has been going on for a hundred years.

At least they don't say Michael Jackson anymore.

Feminism is the politic that has helped me to articulate myself, and queer is my embodied practice of staying alive. But I worry that queer spaces have become places where the illusion of critical thinking hides the policing of thought. I don't want any team to win, I want to end winning.

One thing about beauty is that when it lies in the eyes of the beholder, it lies. Hollow, hallowed, horny, hope. To open the mouth wider, is this a song or a scream, a yawn or a gasp for breath? If I say I write in order to stay alive, this is more than a rhetorical gesture, it's a strategy that has worked.

The people who reached out to me when I moved to Seattle, one thing I didn't mention was disability. This was one way we connected. Some of us because we were living it, and some of us because we knew the need, we were feeling it, we were feeling it together.

Have you ever gone to the park with a group of friends, and then you're so tired you lie in silence in the sun, trying to pass out until you gain enough energy to speak? I mean I'd always connected through speaking, but to connect through not-speaking, this felt like a different kind of camaraderie. I'd found a new group of friends who understood how to politicize queerness through disability. I mean it felt soft. It felt calm. It felt like maybe this was why I came to Seattle, how these people knew me through my work, and there was a gentleness there.

Maybe community accountability is a gasp for breath. If I say it's not my story to tell, then you know I'm not telling the whole story. Someone who we'd all respected, and loved—a transmasculine prison abolitionist with a childlike smile, someone who gave great hugs—he had abused multiple partners, and, while abusing them, had manipulated them into taking care of him, his childhood trauma, over and over. Four of his ex-lovers came together to share their stories—they found a facilitator who believed in transformative justice. After several months they decided they wanted to intervene. They invited six people they all trusted into this process, six people who were friends with their abuser, and I was one of those six people. Our job was to hold our friend accountable without causing more harm. Not to push him away, but to bring him in. They didn't want to talk to him—that was our role.

So the eleven of us met—the four ex-lovers, one facilitator, and six people on the accountability team. I was so excited after that meeting. Everyone was so thoughtful, and grounded—we were complex in our responses and layered in our understanding, not afraid to admit what we didn't know, to ask questions, to grasp at the perils and possibilities. We were in this together, building something deeper than rhetoric.

And we were going deep right away. This was what I wanted, right?

Here is the gap where I don't know what I can tell you, so I'll just leave this gap.

Eventually I had to pull out of the process because it was taking a toll on my body, all the secrets, everything I had to hold in. When you block out trauma, it just becomes more trauma, we all knew this. Which was why we were trying to intervene.

But at a certain point it felt like those of us on the accountability team were just supposed to remain silent, to do what we were told, to be accessories in a process that wasn't really ours. Was there accountability in this accountability process?

Near the end of my involvement, we met with a second facilitator who said something to the accountability team like: You need to listen to survivors. And I was stunned. How dare she assume that we were not also survivors.

He was a survivor too, reliving his own trauma—trying or maybe not trying to change, I think it went back and forth. But trauma is not an excuse. You can be a survivor and accountable, this I knew.

Critical analysis can be a form of intimacy, but so often our lives get stuck between the analytical and the felt, the embodied and the structural. But also in this process I saw how the intimacy itself could be a trap. The way he wielded his trauma as control.

How do you unwind the damage, when you're still so damaged? Maybe I still don't know the answer. Maybe the dream of queer is just another consumer mirage. Maybe we need to bury the dream in order to imagine something else. But how do you bury a dream, without burying yourself?

How people say such beautiful things in mourning. How the absence of these beautiful things in life makes so many of us want to die, in these queer worlds we've made for our living. And when this happens it feels like a shock, but also an expectation. And when we die, if we don't disappear from the record then we become notorious or commodified in ways that mask more than they reveal.

Sometimes we give up, and in giving up we hope that we won't always—I mean if we're not quite giving up. When nostalgia creates a life never lived to replace a life, another form of death, this just goes on and on. Replacing the real death with the false life, and this is how people imagine hope. Why we can never feel hopeful.

Remembering when the goal was to make popular culture irrelevant, so we could create something else. Remembering when the goal was creating unpopular culture. I'm pretty sure this is a parody of a construction site—the only problem is they're constructing a real building. The cult of responsibility, and the culture of irresponsibility—are these the same thing?

When someone says equality, I just hear bombs. If war is the disorder, isn't post-traumatic stress a logical response? One problem with cooking is there's always more cooking— I don't think anyone has ever adequately addressed the question of how it can take so long to do nothing.

I was a faggot before I was a queen, and what I mean is this—on the playground they saw something in my eyes, in my gestures, a kindness, and they needed to squash it. These were boys, and occasionally a girl in league with the boys. This is still the way it is today, decades after the playground, except now the boys are fags. And the girls in league with the boys are also fags.

When I say I was a faggot before I was a queen, what I mean is that I didn't know. I didn't know what they saw. And once I did know, I didn't know how they saw it. Later I realized it was gender they saw and not desire, but can gender be an expression of desire too. I know we're supposed to see the two as separate, but what about when they aren't so separate?

It was always the girls who gave me shelter, but also they were looking for shelter. I mean we gave each other shelter. So I was always told I was a girl, and told I could never be a girl. So many faggots have this story to tell, and yet there are so few spaces where we can embrace it.

When I say I was a faggot before I was a queen, I should say that queer was the word and the world I stepped into as soon as I got away, and faggot was what I embraced once I knew I needed to reject even more. I remember the time my parents came with me to an ACT UP meeting in San Francisco, when I was 19, and they said they were impressed by how passionate everyone was, how eloquent, but why did they have to talk that way? You don't talk that way.

They meant the lisp and the swish, and that's when I realized I was still holding back. I was holding onto the gestures I'd cultivated in high school, counterculture as a way to camouflage femininity, a toughness that said I didn't care what anyone thought. So when my parents said you don't talk that way, and they meant it as a compliment, I was embarrassed.

I remember the first time I walked through the Castro, with my friend Denise in 1992, after driving cross-country. Everyone had said this is where you need to go, to find everything. But when we got there, all we found was that we didn't matter. There were no dykes, so that meant no Denise, and all the fags were busy trying to fit into the exact type of masculinity that was everything I despised. And that was the end of the Castro, the end of the Castro for me.

At least there was a gay bookstore, A Different Light, and there was always some flaming queen or gender-bending diva reigning at the front counter—and honey, those girls recognized me. I would never have said it then, but I was terrified of each of them in different ways. I was terrified they would see me, and I was terrified they wouldn't.

First, there was Tommi Avicolli Mecca—I can't remember when we first started talking about politics, probably it was when I brought in flyers for an ACT UP protest and after that I'd run into Tommi on the street and she'd talk a mile a minute about everything from her activism in Philadelphia in the '70s to San Francisco's current war on the poor and maybe a song she was writing about it all. And then there was Joan Jett Blakk, who ran for President on the Queer Nation ticket—she liked to talk about her Chanel suits, and since I was in queer worlds before gay I didn't really understand that she was joking. And then Justin Vivian Bond would throw over a compliment about the constantly shifting colors of my hair, or my earrings and outfits, and sometimes I would see V out at the dyke clubs too.

These girls were performers too—Tommi at Josie's Juice Joint, Joan Jett Blakk as part of Pomo Afro Homos, and Vivian as part of Kiki and Herb. They were all legends of a different sort, reading—and reading books. And then there was Betty. She was the one I was most confused by, because she just looked like the standard preppy gay man, so preppy it felt like New England more than West Coast, but then as soon as she opened her mouth, she could outdo anyone.

Most of my bookstore days were spent in the Mission at Modern Times, which was more radical and feminist than A Different Light, but it was at A Different Light that I discovered *Steam*, the journal that promoted public sex for fags. Sure, all of my first consensual sexual experiences were in public bathrooms when I was in high school, over and over and over again, but this was something I thought I had to overcome, a legacy of shame that I needed to banish. But *Steam* reveled in the glory of glory holes and beaches and tea rooms and back rooms and sex clubs like these were the ideal places for transcendence. It helped me to realize that my desire didn't have to have bounds, that part of what it meant to be queer was to reject propriety in every form. I didn't have to hide anything.

Or, that was the goal. It still is—for me, anyway.

So I'm thinking about generations, and regeneration. I lived in San Francisco at three different times—first in the early-nineties, then briefly in the mid-nineties, and then from the end of 2000 until the end of 2010. I'm starting to understand the older queens who looked at my bellbottoms in 1992 with bemusement. It's that dislocating sense that something you remember from your past now means something entirely different, if it means anything. In the early-nineties, everyone was telling me I should have been in San Francisco in the '70s, but since I was born in the '70s that just seemed so far away. And because of AIDS it felt unimaginable. But now, when I talk about my moments of formation in the early-'90s, I realize that's even further from the present than the '70s were from my emergence into queer worlds. The difference between longing and belonging is why I write.

I'm joking with Andy about the unicorn as the universal symbol of queer resistance and the way these regurgitated images pop up as supposedly authentic, cutesy, sweet and sublime representations of nothing that wants to be something, or maybe something that wants to be nothing. Which is worse? Go ahead—let's copy that thing those other people copied and then we'll talk about how isn't it such a coincidence that we've all been thinking about unicorns and big chunky '70s fonts and pointy rainbows at the same time, moving downhill in our short-shorts borrowed from someone else's disco jubilee.

Andy sent me a picture from Paris in the springtime, not so dramatic as it sounds because she lives in London, the lighting is great and the green of trees in the background and of course I notice she's modeling the '70s clone facial hair currently de rigueur for big-city contemporary gay worldliness. And she says I knew you would mention that. But then she tells me she went to a movie about gay male desire set in current-day San Francisco, and everyone in the audience was working the same facial hair, and she just wanted to go home right away and shave it all off.

There are ways of experiencing intimacy that are about sharing and caring, and there are ways of experiencing intimacy that are about sharing and caring about the moments when we want to die, just from watching something that's supposed to represent what we care about. The ways these hackneyed representations swirl around you until you're surrounded by sludge, and I'm not just talking about that unicorn in your tan corduroys. The sludge of what we were supposed to be, what we will never be, what we still might desire in moments when we let down our guard. Andy says it was porn, and it would be fine if we were watching it in a porn theater, because then we could start jerking off, but we weren't in a porn theater.

But I wonder if that's a critique of the movie itself, or a critique of the possibilities the movie will never provide, and whether that's the same thing. Because why not start jerking off, all of us in our tan corduroys with these vapid images hailed as art and progress and experience and that big big lollipop that gets stuck to your tongue, a deliberate removal of content passing as consent.

When you break the lollipop in your mouth, the sugar in your teeth might remain there for a while, so eventually you chew on your teeth instead, searching for sweetness. A lollipop is not the same thing as a piece of chewing gum. A piece of chewing gum is not the same thing as everything that sticks to it. Everything that sticks to a piece of chewing gum is not the same thing as the sidewalk where you step on a piece of chewing gum.

What will I remember, and what will I forget. And what will I use a question mark for. And what will I question.

And what will I think of desire. And what will I think. And what will I desire. And what will I imagine. And will I imagine desire. And what will I think of this imagination.

And what will I think of this.

And what will I grasp. And what will I hold. And what will help. And who will I know. And who will I help. And who will I hold. And who will I grasp.

And what will I hope. And what will I hope to grasp. And what will hold hope. And who will hold. And how will I hold hope.

Sure, sometimes I wonder about the possibilities for communal celebration, radical engagement, and sexual splendor of the 1970s, but of course I've also learned the limitations that existed then that do not exist now, or do not exist in the same ways. The opposite of nostalgia is truth. Radical queer worlds in the early-'90s may not have been as binary as the gay and lesbian worlds of the 1970s, but we still had conversations about who could or could not belong that would now seem shockingly outdated.

Everything changes fast in queer worlds, and when I returned to San Francisco in 2000 after four years living elsewhere, suddenly the hottest thing you could possibly be was a tranny—yes, that was the word we used. Tranny meant you were taking things too far—and, honey, you were going to take things further. Tranny meant bring on the messiness, and make it messier. Tranny meant flaunting complication in the face of everyone who wanted to blend in, an excess of gender pushing through either/or norms to declare an allegiance to everything and nothing. As an identity, it could be political or apolitical, fiercely grounded or twirling out into space. Some held onto it to float away, and others to confront hypocrisy. Was there fetishism? Yes. Were there hierarchies? Absolutely. So there were limitations in trying to think beyond limitations, but does this mean we should stop trying?

Part of the dream of queer is that it potentially has no opposite. Straight is the opposite of gay. Queer is a rejection of both.

Queer was one of the first words that spoke to me as the dream I needed in order to survive. I don't know if trans is the same as queer, I mean I know it is and I know it isn't—I know there can be a gloriousness to the potential of trans as a reimagining beyond conventional gender expectations. If queer laid my foundations, a trans analysis rearranged the structures and gave me the space to breathe again. Transgender: to bend, mend, extend, and transcend.

The explosion of trans identities in the early-2000s challenged my own assumptions, including the assumptions that once felt like challenges, and it wasn't just the trans-feminine spectrum that gave me hope in fluidity. I'd always believed that masculinity could only be the enemy, but then there were the trans fags who showed me something beyond the predetermined, a masculinity negotiated and transformed, a flamboyance through choosing a bodily language of one's own making. A freedom, but not a freedom from accountability.

The meanings of queer and trans are constantly shifting—this is part of the allure. At once identities that declare an end to borders, and identities that constantly build walls, challenging enough to derail conversations and at the same time empty enough to use in the name of a TV show or nonprofit. One problem with the politics of representation is that often it's about who is represented, but not what.

I'm not saying we don't ever need an us and them. I know this is how many of us find one another, dance with the scars into arms that might hold not only to harm. I don't think there always needs to be an invitation to join us, I don't think this has to be the case, but I do think this should always be an option. I do think a world without borders is a dream we must hold onto—personally, politically, intimately, explosively, expressively.

There is incredible beauty to the naming and claiming so often found in these worlds, but also there's a frightening territorialism. I don't want to become the cops, I want to end policing in all its forms. This is the dream that queer and trans worlds have helped me to imagine.

And yet there's still so much policing. Here I come back to the assertion that trans is about gender, not sexuality, and I realize maybe that's part of the problem. Because in the spaces where the fullness of my self-expression is allowed, there's rarely the opportunity for my desire to be met, and in the spaces where my desire is met there is rarely space for the rest of me.

In the past, the spaces that allowed me to imagine a future, a future for me or anyone like me, these were almost always created by queer women, and people refusing female socialization to create something else. There were always a few fags and queens and trannies and others leaving mandatory masculinity behind for feminine glory, but we were in the minority and this made sense because how many male-socialized people ever do the work to figure a way out? But in Seattle it's like we barely exist at all in politicized queer spaces. Maybe this shouldn't matter if these spaces aren't for us anyway. Maybe they never were. Maybe queer doesn't include us, or not in the way that means everything. Maybe everything is never everything. I don't know how to express this logically, but I feel like my body will never have a home.

Sometimes I feel like maybe I'm fading away, one day I'll wake up and it will just be that gray between day and night, that hovering of everything between. That blinking of eyes into somewhere else, and not the harshness of stomach tension pushing my insides out, my insides in, not the obliteration of the crash but the softness of the glide. The world we try to make into our own, even as it makes us into the people we don't want to hate, but do, so often we do and we hope for more, consciously and unconsciously trying to get somewhere that maybe we've never known.

Outside, there's a girl gang of shirtless boys jogging in their underwear—is this the new wave of violent crime that everyone's talking about? A mannequin wearing a brightly-colored, dramatically-layered, cartoonish outfit, labeled Street Style, by Anonymous, in a museum show displaying outfits made by exclusive designers that all cost several thousand dollars each. Was there a time when creativity didn't feel like such a desperate act of self-preservation?

One problem with language is that it's still language. I'm wondering if queer will ever become something that holds as much as it harms—will we ever actualize our rhetoric? If queer is a dream that we don't have to die in order to go on living. What would it mean to create a community of care, and have I ever really witnessed this?

This cab driver says what is it with these people, they think they live in a city but this is just a big suburb. I like this cab driver. He says there were three guys in the back seat, laughing about something, but what were they laughing about, they weren't even talking to one another—just sitting with their phones in their hands, texting back and forth. The people here, he says, they don't know how to be people anymore.

One problem with narrative is there's always a master. If dreams are literal, and we are literally dreaming, then what is a dream? When I was 12, I went to a sleep-away camp in West Virginia where there were a bunch of kids from Florida—there was a hailstorm in August, and they thought it was their first snow. I could never be part of other kids' celebrations, anyway.

The feeling of saying I love you to someone for the first time in a way that means comfort, and is this hope or help or helplessness? I'm just so sick of friendships that get stuck somewhere between mutual expressions of commitment, and the other person's next relationship. What does it mean to love when this is all it means?

Adrian and I walk into the bar, and while he's ordering a drink the hottest guy there waves me over—he says how come I don't know you, do I know you, let me add you on Facebook. He's touching me already, complimenting my sweater. He says it reminds him of someone's sofa. Of course he's on a date.

I'm stuck between losing the hope for connection in the places and spaces I used to believe in, and wondering how to find that connection in the spaces I will never believe in. Going into worlds I already know are corrupt, in order to find what isn't. A body without politic, or a politic without a body, this is not a choice I want to make. Some people invoke the search for pleasure as pleasure in the search. But how is there pleasure if there's no pleasure?

Knowing you will never escape, and then you do, but does your body ever really figure this out? Thunder is an understatement—it's the sky meeting the earth, and somehow everything's more alive. Maybe not everything, but everything you can feel. Sometimes it's hard to write when you're in the moment. Because you're in the moment. I wanted to tell you about walking into the bar—when was it? Almost two weeks ago. Was that the last time? It feels like it's been too long.

Confession: sometimes I write in present tense, but I'm not actually there. I mean now Adrian and I go to the bar together—the second time I went there, or the second time I went there, but not just for the photo booth, Adrian spotted me, and said: Mattilda, what are you doing at Pony? He'd been to my book launches over the years, and he reached out when I moved to Seattle, and we exchanged numbers, but that was on Facebook, and I hate Facebook, so when Adrian didn't call I didn't call him. But then when I ran into him at Pony, he said if you ever need someone to go out with—and so now that's what we do. We walk through Cal Anderson on the way there, so I can lean against trees to even out my body, and stretch on the jungle gym. It's one way to appreciate the rain.

Sometimes when Adrian starts to get drunk, she asks me to point out everyone in the bar who I would go home with, and I kind of like playing this game because no one's ever asked me to play before. Or maybe they did, but I thought it was tired. I mean it is tired, but we're at a gay bar—there's no way to avoid tired. I wonder whether Adrian's flirting with me, and I wonder whether I'm flirting with him, and maybe this is part of the game. Then Evan walks in, and he's grabbing me all over. He's the one I told Adrian I would do anything for, and I can tell we could go home together if I stay, but I can't stay because it's getting too late. If I stay too late then I won't be able to sleep, and then my life will be over. Of course I'm that fragile. What happens to the moment, if you're not in the moment?

The feeling of not being able to exist without not really existing. I can go outside, and hope the air will clear my head, but then there's my head again, without air. What does it mean to open? I refuse to allow any flower analogies. By refusing to allow them, I allow them.

I hate waking up in the middle of a dream. And yet this is how we live our lives. We're on the side of a road that isn't really a road, I mean it's blocked off. Or we're on the side of a road that is really a road. But actually neither of these roads are really roads because we're in a park. So you can't say two roads diverged. But you can still be part of manifest destiny, I wish I wasn't but I am and that's probably the best way to describe gay cruising.

What happened to the dream of desire creating something else, that's what I'm wondering. Michael wants to make a historical monument sign mourning the loss of the park as a cruising site, but he's never even cruised the park. I say why not make it happen instead. And he says there are only ugly guys there. And when I say all of us are ugly, he says not you. But can I get distracted by a compliment?

Remember Follow the Leader—that was a critique of leadership, right? Why does it feel like no one else learned this lesson?

Now I'm in the other space. This one has rooms, but not room. I'm walking in circles which are actually squares, and then I stop. And then I'm walking in circles which are actually squares. The moment between the end and the beginning, that's what I want to convey— something about how the music stops, in this case I mean literally, the music stops and then the whole place is darkness and I wish I could say groaning or moaning but mostly just quiet and a creak here and there, the flush of the toilet. I'm studying the blackboard over the urinal where people usually write things like BB in 108 but the board's just been erased so all you see is the way the black surface is peeling off and I wonder if that makes it harder to write but I try and can't tell. Maybe I'm covering the blackboard in little hearts or maybe just two hearts or maybe there are no hearts at all, because this is a sex club.

So the most important thing is when I'm changing back into my clothes, and I say to the guy next to me in the locker room: Why does everyone at a gay bathhouse act like they're straight?

What do you mean, he says, like he's straight.

If desire is what makes sex possible, then what makes the sex that makes desire impossible? There's a probiotic powder designed for anal insertion called the colon-izer, I did not even make this up. And then there's the intersection between colonialism and restaurant reviews. Not to mention the intersection between restaurant reviews and gentrification, which is also about colonialism. Maybe that's why food writing is so popular—it's like writing about food releases the reviewer of the obligation to think about any structural issue deeper than taste buds.

The requirement of the dead audience is its own kind of violence, making us silence ourselves in order to experience public engagement. Emptying presence in order to be present. Now I'm just present in all the pain from sitting still, that's how my body works. Or doesn't work.

That sudden moment when you feel like you can't exist in the world, it's just not possible. Of course I could've gotten up during the reading, but I was feeling the pressure of not wanting to seem rude. This always happens. But still I'm ready to go dancing—I'm out in the world in the right outfit, and we're only a few blocks away.

But then no one else wants to go anymore, and Graham, Adrian's boyfriend, says the DJ isn't even starting until after I need to go to bed—and even if I stay up that late then the smoke machine will be on. And that's when I get so sad, I just crash through the floor while I'm standing there like I might still be able to speak.

We go upstairs to look at books, there are so many horrible gay books. Someone's described as a pioneering activist because he testified against Don't Ask Don't Tell while he was in the military. A supermodel came out, I don't know when. Or why. Marriage this and marriage that. The liberal pundit saying now we need more, more what, more marriage. And then I find a book that I really love, and I talk about it for a while so I won't seem like I hate everything.

In other words, I hate everything. And then Adrian says he's feeling so tired anyway—oh well, time for drinks. And I know that I'm utterly alone.

I want to be out in the world, and I want to feel pleasure. I want to feel connected. Instead I find myself leaning against a tree, and then leaning into it, letting my body relax so that maybe there's something left to learn that won't hurt me.

So many people have written about alienation, and yet we still keep feeling it. Just as I'm inserting that probiotic enema, the plumber knocks at the door. This must be a metaphor. But sometimes the best thing about writing is the way you feel afterwards. Like there finally might be space in the sky. Like there finally might be space for more writing. Like there finally might be more sky.

Evan and I go to a party described as a building takeover, in the old house where I used to go to therapy. Every room is filled with art except my therapist's former office, which is locked. It isn't really a takeover, because the organizers have the key, and the landlord's permission. Too many people think displacement is inevitable.

Evan wants to know what I would do if I owned all the beautiful old houses on Capitol Hill that are about to be torn down, wouldn't I sell them to developers? But I still want to make out with him. It could've happened the other night, but it was too late for me and now I guess it's too late for him. He says he can't date right now, because of his ex-boyfriend, the way he still feels. We're not talking about dating, but I'm trying to touch him in the way he was touching me on that night, and then I feel it, the shift away, his body language.

One good thing about living near the cruising park is that when you lose a mitten at night, you can go back in the morning to find it. Is this hunger or exhaustion, I don't know. True story: I'm looking for a bandaid I lost in a pot of steamed kale. Will I ever recover from recovering?

Every bad movie is about trying to get back into a dream you never really had, and I'm still trying to get out of that movie. Sometimes I feel like I spend half the day cooking, and the other half trying to recover from what I ate. I know there's something called restful sleep, because I heard about it in someone else's dreams.

But how strange that walking into a bar can make me feel like desire is a float I can land on. So I mean glide, glide through the air into a body that works. That doesn't need to work. That reaches for the air and finds joy. This is before the smoke machine floods the room and I rush outside to tell Adrian my night is over.

It's a hipster gay bar that sees itself as different, and that's what makes me an item, but also there aren't enough hipster fags in this town to fill the bar, so it rarely becomes sceney in the way that feels like instant suffocation. But then that's also the problem, because a group of 10 arrives and suddenly they own the bar. Especially on weekends, when standard masculinity takes over and I lose any hope of dreaming. Mark thinks they're hot, some of them. Of course some of them are hot, but that's the problem. That's always the problem. The violence of the cops as proof of their necessity.

I'm on the way to Volunteer Park, and someone's trying to catch up with me, and then he does, some gorgeous blonde guy, kind of mod, maybe straight, across the street, saying do you usually wear a different hat? I do, I say, but this is my nighttime hat, because of the cold. And he says what's your name, I see you around the neighborhood all the time, I live in the neighborhood. Mattilda, I say, and he says I'm Elliott.

What are you up to right now, I say, wondering if he wants to join me for this walk, or anything else—he says I'm meeting a friend, and the way he says it makes me think he doesn't want to say girlfriend. Or maybe boyfriend, I'm not sure, but I say I hope I see you soon, and then, just when I turn the corner on Tenth, what am I doing on Tenth, I never take Tenth, too many cars, but just as I turn the corner this big fluffy cat comes running up to me. I could tell you about my trip to Volunteer Park, but really this is the best part.

Adrian loves cats, I should tell Adrian about this cat. His eyes will get big and he'll start to smile like a little kid, and that's what happens with me too, when I see a cat on the street, or especially when I'm petting it. Adrian has a cat in his apartment, but maybe we can be cats too. Maybe we can be cats together.

But also there's the moment when I'm fucking this guy in between two trees, and he says did you come, I say yeah, but I can keep going, and afterwards I think who the hell was that, with all that energy, that masculine drive, suddenly, in a way that feels potentially healing. So maybe that's the best part. But actually it's when I get to the main lawn afterwards, so gorgeous in the dark, and I'm opening my arms to the sky to yell hello like my therapist who isn't my therapist anymore suggested but usually I don't really yell it, don't want to make other people uncomfortable—but now there's no one around except me and the trees.

When someone else's desire is what makes me feel mine, does this mean this is someone else's desire? I'm waiting for Adrian on the patio at the bar, but I'm stuck at a table where everyone's too drunk, friendly in a way that can be fun for a few minutes, but then I'll crash. I see Adrian inside, but she doesn't come out so I'm kind of stuck until I go inside and say let's move out on our own like we need to catch up. So we escape to the back where the patio points out like an arrow into the street and the gorgeous light at dusk isn't even hurting my eyes— Adrian and I are talking in that way that already feels conspiratorial, just the two of us about to launch away.

Back inside, Adrian says he doesn't know how to dance to this music, which is what he always says when it's the music I want to dance to. It's getting close to 10 and I say you'll regret it if you don't dance now, although what I really mean is that I'll regret it—and then we're dancing together at last, and at one point I say is it okay if I fall on you? And Adrian says you can fall on me any-time. And I take that in all its possibilities.

And when Adrian goes to the bathroom, this girl I met earlier starts throwing down voguing moves, yes I'm in and out of her hands so graceful windmill I'm falling into the beat we're catching each other a mix of abandoning and partnership and now it's time to go. I mean for me. Adrian says he's leaving too, doesn't want to stay too late, so we're off to my invented club called Mirrorama at the corner of Pine and lucky Thirteenth, which is really just the mirrored windows on an abandoned warehouse and I ask if it feels different on the different sides. Adrian says which side do you like better? I say I can't pick favorites, but that side is like a calm breeze after a devastating storm, and this one is like a party where the lights are flickering on and off.

Across the street, two guys look like they're about to make out or break up, I'm not sure which, but then when they make out I'm yelling yes, that's what we were waiting for—and this is when I think I can love it here. Down through Cal Anderson, and after stretching on the playground we're lying on the Astroturf, because I'm wearing white patterned pants, and Adrian's wearing his white Sinead O'Connor T-shirt, so we don't want any grass stains. Look at how the clouds are moving, I could fall asleep here. Adrian says remember the other night in Volunteer Park when we did kind of fall asleep, and I do, my head resting on his chest, or between chest and armpit, and I'm thinking about how we're building a relationship that says you can fall on me anytime.

But it's hard to believe in a relationship if you never know whether the other person is going to call you back. You prepare for that moment, hold yourself in, even when you're trying to hold on. You're present, and yet there's a lack of presence.

On the bus, this guy has a good tune:

Gentrifi-ca-tion

Sublimi-na-tion

Abomi-na-tion

Obey the na-tion

Oblite-ra-tion

When people are always flaky, I know they're flaky, so I know not to depend on them. We can still be friends, but it will only go so far. But what do I do when the people I depend on are flaky?

Whenever someone describes a Hollywood movie like it's talking about an important subject, I know that subject is lost. But some people are in love with what they can't say. Panic as the body stopping. The body a stop. Stopping the body.

Sex when you feel shut down, maybe it will make you feel something else. Sex to escape thinking. Sex to escape thinking about sex. Maybe what I'm saying is that if someone else's desire is the desire that makes me feel hopeful, is this really hopeful?

But then this guy is fucking me inside a rhododendron bush—I'm trying to hold on but really there's nothing to grab onto, except this place of openness, literally my asshole I mean I'm getting fucked in the park and my body is finally an open door. And then afterwards he says he doesn't understand why people are always ashamed, what is there to be ashamed of—why would anyone spend so much time trying to hook up on the internet, when they could be here?

Maybe now I can write about Adrian, the physical sensation of safety when I'm around him, a gravitational pull. Maybe safety is the wrong word—I just want to know that when we make plans, he'll actually show up. I want to know that when he says he'll call, he'll actually call. Is that too much to ask, too much to ask from a close friend?

I'm so sick of relationships that don't get to the places where they should—I want to believe that a relationship can last. I want to believe that people who don't believe in prioritizing dating over friendship will actually put this into practice.

I don't like arguing anymore, I mean not just to argue. Although maybe I spend too much effort avoiding it, avoiding it with my friends. But then everyone ends up disappearing anyway. I don't just want islands of closeness without a connecting structure, I want relationships that I feel in my body as cellular possibility.

Yes, I'm getting fucked again, this time in the cedar grove with winding old trees that have trunks so wide they angle out from the ground like living boats. But who decided that baby-powder-scented petroleum jelly was allowed? Luckily I have my own lube. At first I was going to fuck him, but then he did that thing where he leaned on the tree like there was no one around, I mean not even me, and I'll never be able to fuck anyone that way.

But I like the way he grabs me around the waist, and then asks if he can come in the condom. There's more support from the trees than the rhododendron bush, so I can even try different angles, feel into exactly what's opening.

Probably for all of us there's a time when we feel like we're living out of time. For me that time is now. I refuse to text because I want to feel, and is this outdated, this way of feeling? This feeling that I want to feel something that isn't just feeling stuck. This feeling that maybe I can build a text of my own that will allow me to express what I can't express.

The quality of my life has significantly declined since the social norm of talking on the phone to friends has shifted from a common assumption to a rare commodity. I can't help thinking this is just another way of giving into distance. How people act like their fear of talking on the phone is something so unique and they don't know why, but actually it's a dominant cultural norm. Or people embrace the norm, and act offended when you question it. It makes sense to me that people who grew up texting might be skittish about talking on the phone, but then there are people older than me who will say they've always been afraid. And maybe that's true. I just wish people had stopped talking on the phone in order to see one another more often, but unfortunately it's just to never see one another.

I'm on the street, and someone cruises me, and he looks down at his phone, and I imagine he's looking to see if I'm there. When they tear down a beautiful old house, and replace it with a FOR SALE sign in front of the vacant lot—maybe if the next owners have a sense of history, they'll name the new building after what they tore down. I don't want to get used to relationships that don't really matter to me, relationships without a continuum, relationships where I'm facilitating the whole thing, relationships where I'm the only one calling, relationships that aren't really relationships.

Maybe when you're younger it's easier to find the friends who will always be there. Because they won't. But also the drive to connect just in order to survive. To create something other than the violence we're escaping. Where does this drive go?

I'm singing about the bee sting that made my whole lower leg swell up, and there's a cute guy up ahead, across from the hospital in his scrubs, walking his dog outside his apartment, so convenient. The dog starts barking at me and he picks it up to show it how nice I am so I'm petting the dog and I catch this guy looking at my chest. I want to say you're cute too, can I pet you, but instead I just touch his shoulder and say have a good night. The next step is just to say it, right? Just say it—what do I have to lose?

Don't tell anyone, but I just looked on craigslist missed connections. When you lack the energy to find the alternatives because you're so exhausted by the lack of alternatives. Adrian's trying to tell me why he doesn't call, but then he says he doesn't want to use that as an excuse. But an excuse for what? How much our relationship means to him, that's what he says, and I get kind of confused. But then I realize he's saying he doesn't want to use that as an excuse for not calling me. Although I kind of want to know how much our relationship means to him—do I need an excuse?

Really I just want to get to the point where we roll glass beads down the hill like marbles, I'm losing my marbles, and then throw the wooden ones onto the highway at the bottom because they're light, they won't break any windows. It's what I wanted to do on my birthday—we made plans to get together, but then Adrian didn't call me back. Letting go of distance in favor of closeness. Letting go of loneliness in favor of hope. Letting go of safety in favor of vulnerability.

No, that's not right. I don't even have safety.

And when you get to the bottom of the hill, before the steps down to Melrose overlooking the highway, you look to the right on Bellevue, and there are sunflowers growing out of the sidewalk—and all these potted plants, leading to an apartment with a ground-level entrance on the side of the building.

I decide to leave a note: I love this little garden, thank you.

When everyone is reading the same thing, does this make it accessible? When no one is reading anything interesting, does this make interesting reading inaccessible? When no one is reading, what are you reading?

There's that moment when you think why am I putting on the same CD again, but then there's the moment when you think how can I ever listen to anything else? There's the part of me that wants to say come on over for dinner, and there's the part of me that doesn't know if I'll ever be ready.

I'm on the bus, sitting next to some guy who's taking up half my seat by spreading his legs, and usually in a situation like this I try to take up as little space as possible, but that always ends up hurting my body so this time I think why not just let my leg rest against his, I mean isn't that what he's doing? And then once I'm doing that I can feel the leg hairs close to my knee, and is my skin touching his skin—no, it's our shorts touching our shorts, and there's something really hot about this, I mean I don't know if it's mutual because I didn't detect anything suggestively gay about him but of course I know that's not what matters.

When I breathe in, he breathes out—that's how close our bodies are. He moves his hands a little, and I want to look over to see if he's hard, but I can't do it without looking like I'm looking. The feeling of his legs against mine, arms pressing into one another too, we're in this together.

Oh, we're getting off at the same stop. We exit the door on opposite sides, and I look over to see if he looks over, but he rushes into the Broadway Market. And it's the rushing that makes me think something was going on—but if he wasn't rushing, then what would I think?

How is it possible to drop an earring on the floor, and never find it again? Somehow I do this all the time. I guess when you put yourself on the no-call list, that's how the telemarketers get your number.

Maybe the best thing that's happened to me this year is that I can finally do a somersault—yes, I'm slowly making my way back to age six. My grandmother still can't believe I don't have a TV. There are some good programs on, she says—let's put it this way: MIND NUMBING—they keep you informed. I'm thinking about the way that integration and segregation often coexist, and when this is the intention. Certainly there's no place for autonomy in this world, which I guess is what autonomy means.

Adrian comes over, and it feels so good just to sit on the sofa for an hour, trying not to let the light hurt my eyes because it's so calming to feel our bodies in contact. Adrian's telling me about listening to Judy Garland—he's looking for one of her albums that's hard to find, how her voice is so raw and true. How he's almost ten years younger than me but he has some of the same female icons as the queens decades older than both of us—Marilyn Monroe, even. Mama Cass. And some actress whose name I can never remember who wrote a memoir about fighting cancer. The way they are all trapped, and fighting. I think that's what it's about—is that what it's about?

How they turn their pain into power in their work is what Adrian says—how to live through pain and what to do with it, how to transform it—whatever I was looking to do, or not do. The first time I heard Mama Cass, Adrian says, I thought I was her in a past life because I felt like a fat woman trapped inside a femme boy's body—I was 11 and I pretended that I already knew all her lyrics, like she could have been me. And when I saw *Beautiful Thing*, when I was 12 or 13, and the soundtrack was the Mamas & the Papas, and I wasn't out yet, but I knew there was this thing I was trying to escape and it was right around the corner, and that's when I started hiding all these heroes of mine, so all the people who already called me gay wouldn't have more ammunition.

But then there's also Miss Piggy, what was it about Miss Piggy? I have to remember to ask about that, but now Adrian's talking about sexual abuse, his brother, how his mother knew but she just said boys will be boys, and now he's crying and I'm holding him and I want to stay present in this vulnerability. How it makes me feel capable. Because I know what to do. This history we share.

When we're saying goodbye, I notice Adrian's hands are cool, which is surprising because usually I'm the one with the cold hands—warm heart, strangers say, but the doctors told me Reynaud's phenomenon, starting when I was 12, not that that matters, and Adrian says: It does matter, because I want to know everything about you.

And this is what matters.

Staying present in desire without losing track of my sense of self. Staying present in my sense of self without losing track of desire. What I like about this guy is that he doesn't seem nervous about being a fag—right when I spot him, he says hi like a normal person. I mean like a person. But he's smoking, and I don't want to get too close so I circle around to see what's happening on the main lawn, and it turns out they're showing Japanese horror movies—I guess that's why there are so many random people around.

Then I circle back, and there's the same guy, but without the cigarette, and we're holding hands on the way to find our secret spot and then we're hugging really hugging and that's especially nice because on my way to the park I was thinking what I really want is a hug, I mean first I thought I wanted to get fucked, and then I thought no, what I really want is a hug, and once in a while we get to have both.

I love the way he pulls me back while he's fucking me, away from the tree so he's the one holding me up and I realize I'm sweating, really sweating in the park I mean is it that hot out, and when he comes he gets really quiet and soft and then I get loud, and when he pulls out he kind of shudders as he takes the condom off. After he finds his phone in the dead spiky leaves, we duck under the holly branches and rejoin the world. I'm petting his shaved head and he loves it, he loves me petting his head. Someone walks by and his gaze turns, I say are you waiting for him—he says no I wouldn't be here if I was.

What about you, he says, and I realize he thinks I'm asking if he has a boyfriend. I give him my number but I figure he won't call. On my way home I'm thinking about how good that was, how connected, and what would that be like somewhere else—it wouldn't be possible in the same way, but what else would?

And I think that's the same guy I met a year ago, he was driving by and he said nice shorts, got out of the car and then we were making out, sucking each other's dicks right there by the road and then someone throwing a ball to her dog was looking in our direction, but we were in the dark, so I didn't think she could see us, but he got scared and pulled up his pants, literally ran to his car and drove away. So it's good to see he's not as scared now.

Sometimes you play the same song so much that you end up hating it, but then one day you wake up thinking: Why don't I play that song anymore? What becomes repetitive and dull, boring and monotonous, the same old thing, a tragedy, jumping off a bridge with the moon up above so bright, no I'm talking about sound not light, the light of sound and suddenly it's off and then on again. I'm talking about my body, up against the oven in the morning and suddenly everything is tingling. Because I wake up thinking about how I'm trying to figure out a new way to exist in a world of fags, a new way to exist in the world.

And, strangely, instead of leading me to the relationships I know I need, suddenly I've mastered the art of getting fucked in the park. I know I need more, but is this a step in the right direction? This guy keeps pushing me to the ground up against one of my favorite sequoia trees—it's a giant in the sky for us, and I wonder why the dirt, but then I realize oh, he's too short to fuck me out here any other way, our bodies wouldn't match. And then I realize I like it in the dirt. And when he grabs my chest, rubs my whole body like that's what he's here for, all of me—or all of my body, anyway—that's when I really feel him fucking me.

So I've finally figured out how to use condoms in the way that means always, now that everyone's talking about abandoning condoms. Of course people were abandoning condoms before, but now this is described as the truly great way of mastering HIV prevention, a pill. The truly great pill made by a right-wing pharmaceutical company that's changing our lives.

I want to feel joyous about PrEP, like something has changed, because I know it's changed something for many people, allowing more freedom for sexual expression without fear they say, although I don't believe the part about without fear. I know that PrEP is saving lives, or at least preventing HIV infection, but I can't exactly feel this, not in the way I'm supposed to.

I'm too disturbed by seeing people I'm vaguely acquainted with becoming marketing tools for a transnational pharmaceutical company. I'm too disturbed by HIV prevention campaigns that talk about ending AIDS without even mentioning a cure.

We only have effective treatment because activists fought the government and drug companies for years. Now people romanticize the early days of ACT UP, but the early days meant everyone was dying. That was where the rage came from, and nothing would have changed without that rage. But now that the industry makes drugs that actually help, many former activists are inside and not out. What was once a movement is now a subsidiary.

I'm watching a movie where the desert is an escape for the deserted. Deserting what deserts you. A movie about

HIV-positive gay men who moved to Palm Springs in the '90s to die, and instead they ended up living. But then someone says: "You stop those medications, you're dead—that's not chronic."

A dominant narrative is always a form of erasure. How many people hide the scars, literal and figurative, in order to conform to what's supposed to be? Yes, we live in a far different world than the one where an HIV diagnosis meant imminent death, but we also live in a world where public demand for a cure is nearly nonexistent.

It's becoming harder to imagine that queers were once nearly united in suspicion of the pharmaceutical industry. Now we're supposed to be grateful for toxic drugs to prevent HIV infection, and toxic drugs to prevent AIDS, so the drug companies keep profiting off our bodies, healthy or sick it doesn't matter as long as they profit.

When I say the word cure, most people look surprised, or they look away—positive or negative, they look away. People talk about PrEP as a new sexual revolution, and there's nothing wrong with a personal health decision in search of affirmation—except when this is defined as activism. A sexual revolution without a political revolution isn't a revolution at all, it's just consumer choice branded as liberation.

Prevention strategies change. I know this. I remember when I used condoms for sucking cock, Kiss of Mint—remember Kiss of Mint? Without a condom, you could lick the shaft, but not the head. And then consensus shifted, and sucking cock became low-risk, and I swallowed as much come as I could get. Is this what it's like now, with a newly acceptable fetish for loads up the ass? I mean a renewed acceptability.

I'm not part of the generation that lost everyone to AIDS, but the generation that only had this to imagine. The one time I came in someone's ass without a condom, I felt like the most horrible person in the world. Even though I knew I was negative. Even though he begged me for it, gave me a big tip, because come is a form of currency, don't we all know that?

There was a time when I would let people fuck me without a condom at first, because that way I could relax, it was the only way there wouldn't be too much pain. And I went to a safer sex workshop in New York around 1998, thinking my life was out of control and what would happen next, and the facilitator said he thought I was managing risk. I didn't get a chance to talk about how anytime someone was teasing my asshole with his dick he would end up fucking me without asking, and what did this mean about consent—does consent even exist in gay male sexual culture?

When I moved back to San Francisco in 2000, and ended up in a sexual relationship for the first time in years, my boyfriend and I made the decision not to use condoms, as long as we used them all the time with everyone else. I made that decision for his safety, so it was easy. But then after our relationship ended, I realized I wanted to make that choice for my own safety. How long ago was that? Over a decade.

For a while I didn't get fucked at all, because I loved that gentle tease of someone's dick against my ass so much, but I knew what it would lead to. So now I've finally figured out a way to use condoms all the time, beyond the pain of initial insertion and into that abandon I've always fantasized about. And I'm not about to give up this new grasp on safety and pleasure and self for someone else's desire, or for some toxic drug my fragile body wouldn't be able to tolerate anyway. How long has PrEP been around? Only two years. A lot can change in two years, but why let go of what's making me stronger, even if now some guys turn away as soon as you mention condoms?

I wish that taking care of yourself wasn't so embedded with consumer choice. What does it take for personal fears to become politicized? And what does it take for this politicization to be replaced by consumer loyalty? Does a craving for normalcy ever disappear, I mean on a large-scale cultural level, or does it just hide temporarily, only to reemerge when opportunity strikes?

In 1996 or 1997, during the first period when I officially lived in Seattle, I worked as an outreach worker for Friend to Friend—our job was to go to bars, and ask the bartenders who the peer leaders were, and educate them about safer sex. If the bartenders didn't identify anyone, which happened most of the time, then we would just stand there with our badges for three hours. We could talk to people about safer sex if they came up to us, which usually only happened if they were smashed and wanted to flirt with one of us, but we weren't supposed to go up to anyone on our own.

Just talk to the ones the bartenders like, and everything will be fine, right? Peer pressure is the way to go. Except that pretty much every horrible thing about gay culture can be traced back to peer pressure. So why do public health campaigns rely on this rather than challenging it?

I worked for Friend to Friend right when protease inhibitors were changing HIV into a more manageable condition for many, but it didn't feel that way yet. I mean that rhetoric didn't even exist, or at least I didn't hear it. Maybe Gay City had a town hall about the new drugs, but I didn't go. I never went to Gay City events then, even though I was always curious. Maybe it was the word gay, which felt too limiting—I was worried I wouldn't have any way to relate.

Or maybe I didn't go because I had Andy, who would call me every day and say what are you up to? Trying to leave the house. And then she would come over. Or I would call her, when she was trying to get out of bed, and drag her out so we could go to dinner. Dinner meant we would talk about every detail in our lives, everything that was overwhelming so then maybe it wouldn't be so over-whelming. But also we could just feel it, just feel it together and that was that.

When we were done talking, we would go out for cock-tails, so we could keep talking—we were both alienated by the bland middle-class values and lowest common denomi-nator attitude of Seattle gays, but at least we could throw some shade of our own by making up code names for the girls we thought were the most tired, and talking about them right in their faces. And then going to Basic Plumbing after the bars closed, swaying to the beat in search of the high from a sudden hookup, that moment of connection in those dark hallways I already knew so well.

Andy and I were a couple in the way that always felt the most comfortable for me, by which I mean that neither of us acknowledged we were a couple. It wasn't sexual or even physical, but there was a loyalty and a camaraderie that continues to this day—even though Andy has lived in Europe for the past 15 years. Still, when we talk on the phone it's back, this sense that we're in a relationship that will last. Why is that so hard to find now?

Maybe it's something about when you first have the freedom to create your own terms, how everyone is searching, and 15 or 20 years later there are so few who are still searching for the same things. I remember when I first came to Seattle to escape San Francisco, in 1994, when I was 20. I was staying with JoAnne for a month, and she lived just up the hill from where I live now. Actually I walk by there all the time, I study the building to see what's changed. Which is what I do with every building, but it's not like every building changed me.

That first time I came to Seattle, I carried *The Courage to Heal* around like it might save me, and sometimes it did, so maybe that's why JoAnne and I started talking about surviving rape and crystal and hopelessness right away—this conversation that went on and on and allowed our bodies to breathe, to breathe for the first time, that's what we were in the process of doing.

I shared a bed with JoAnne for a month in Seattle, and there was so much joy there, so much joy in our rage. I remember her body and how it felt like comfort, safety, a release from harm—when we held each other, we didn't need to hold anything back. That month with JoAnne was the first time I understood what it meant to relax—I'd always thought that if I let go, there would be nothing left.

But I was fleeing the city that had made and unmade me, so I needed to go back. JoAnne moved down soon after, and then San Francisco became the dream again because it was our dream together. If I say that JoAnne died not much more than a year later, you know how time doesn't work to describe a lifetime together. We were out of time, and we were in it. I was living in Boston when JoAnne got strung out on heroin, I mean she'd started before but I believed her when she said it wouldn't become a problem. Crystal was the problem, we both agreed about that.

But the problem was also the scene of outcast dykes reveling in performative destruction that I'd once believed in—I thought we were creating our own world to undo the damage, but then it felt like there was only more damage. Maybe I could leave, because I wasn't a dyke. But JoAnne wanted so much to be a part of this world that shunned her when she became a junkie. So then what did she have left?

I moved back after JoAnne died, and I moved back again after that. Eventually I had to write a book called *The End of San Francisco*, because I kept believing in those same worlds, or different versions of them, over and over I believed. Until everything just felt like loss.

If all you feel is loss, then eventually you will no longer feel.

Sometimes I miss that bed so much, that bed I shared with JoAnne in Seattle, when we were just learning how to breathe. I want to breathe like that again.

That physical feeling of comfort is the thing I've always craved, once I stopped cultivating distance in order to survive. So when Derek and Zee moved to Seattle in 1996, I should have had that again, right? They were the ones who allowed me to feel for the first time that sex and love didn't have to be separate. I know we're supposed to be confused about the separation, but the connection had always been more confusing to me.

Derek and I were almost boyfriends, until I met Zee across the country at an ACT UP protest in 1993. When I got back to San Francisco, Derek had found someone else to fill that role—we never talked about it, since neither of us believed in monogamy, but I think he found that boyfriend so fast because he was scared I was going to leave him. But still we had a commitment to one another, it was us against the world and that was what mattered to me.

Zee became my first boyfriend after love letters from Michigan in envelopes full of photocopied art that I still have in my file cabinet with all my other letters, remember letters? And then Zee moved to San Francisco and I could feel my body shifting, something inside that meant safety but also it meant a raw vulnerability and then we were breaking down. And breaking up. And breaking down. And breaking up. You know the story, right? It's how I ended up in Seattle that first time, sharing JoAnne's bed. When this was what you would do with friends, you would just share. Two years and three cities later, I mean later for me, Derek and Zee were in a relationship, and they were moving to Seattle so we could be in a relationship together.

But then they were living just up the hill from me, and I never saw them. Their relationship was falling apart, and they were trying to hold it together, which was always the way with them, but I didn't know this yet. All I have to prove that they were here is a picture of the two of them lying in my bed, facing away from me.

As a measure of my loneliness, let me tell you that sometimes I'm jealous when people pet the stuffed animal I keep on my sofa. Remembering when the phone was the phone, and now people are surprised when it still is. But the myth of a golden age prevents us from creating a golden age.

You know when you love a song so much, but you don't realize it's a cover? And then you hear the original, and you think: What is this shit? I used to believe in this thing called queer. Wait, I still believe? I can't believe it.

When someone says human beings shouldn't be treated like cattle, I think cattle shouldn't be treated like cattle. Walking down the street, sometimes I think a fire hydrant is a person, and sometimes I think a sign is a person, and sometimes I think a person is a person. The problem with language is that it's always broken.

An unbroken text doesn't allow context. An unbroken context isn't enough text. Or am I romanticizing experience? Please don't allow the drawbridge.

Knock knock.

Who's there?

This isn't the only thing language is for.

But I'm back in the park again. I didn't think I wanted to have sex, but then I'm pissing on this huge tree with a trunk that's so many different textures that bark isn't enough to describe it—don't call me a dog, okay I'm a dog if this means I can experience joy without the cage. I'm watching the way the shadows are moving under the cedar tree right by the road where people sometimes have sex, and then I can't help it, there I am under that tree my desire the breeze but there's no one there.

How much context do you need for breath—I want to pause here, to allow for feeling. Do I go back to the guy who fucked me in the rhododendron bush, to tell you he was wearing a Hawaiian shirt? Maybe that's what I liked about him, at first. And what about the guy who fucked me in the dirt, making my legs ache right at the groin for several days after—should I mention his rotten teeth, a few of them, when I saw that the first time I thought poverty, but now I realize addiction. Addiction plus poverty is not exactly a pretty sight, but you don't notice, except when he smiles. Sometimes he understands what I'm saying, and sometimes he doesn't—is this a language barrier?

Maybe I'm just trying not to call my mother. I don't want to tell her how she makes me feel. Of course we're talking about money, something she's offered and may never give, not what I want anyway, which is security. I have security because my grandmother died, my father's mother, she left me money, it's what I live on. But I want the next level, the level that means this will not end. This is where disability has left me, I will use that word even if I'm scared of it. Scared to claim it. Scared it will claim me.

When I'm sitting on the sofa with Adrian, and we're both so tired that we're talking about my fan, how it cools the air by redirecting it, rather than just blowing out, and he says I bet your plants must really like all that air. Adrian's wearing his new Miss Piggy t-shirt, with puffy red shoulders and bedazzled gems, and I say oh, I wanted to ask you, what is it about Miss Piggy?

And Adrian says I always loved Miss Piggy, she helped me get through some of the hardest parts of my child-hood—I was Miss Piggy for Halloween when I was three years old. She was so femme but also very butch, these conflicting identities, that's how I would describe her now, with these queer terms, but when I was 3 to 11 I would dissociate and pretend I was Miss Piggy while my brother molested me. If I couldn't fight my brother off, in the end, when I felt like Miss Piggy, I felt like I hadn't totally lost myself—and now I just feel so pathetic, I mean she wasn't even real.

Adrian's crying again, and I'm saying that's not pathetic at all, it's how you survived. I'm petting his neck and watching the tears, how tears can allow so much closeness and I don't want to underemphasize trauma but also there's the way we share our stories and they open us up. How maybe Adrian said something similar before, but it wasn't so direct. How the directness allows me to feel it. How it's here in the room but we're still here too—it's moving through us and we're moving through it.

And then Adrian calls to sing me a song, Belly with my name instead of the name that's actually in the song, because I told him I listened to it with JoAnne—it was her music, which is also his music. And Adrian says: I didn't know if you would answer—I thought maybe I would sing into your voicemail and then get cut off and keep re-recording.

And this is what a relationship means to me. Although I'm not sure about "Mattilda carried a rifle"—what do you mean a rifle, I would never carry a rifle.

Adrian remembers a blog post I wrote a long time ago about listening to Belly with JoAnne, saying every song was about abuse or shopping in a grocery store, and it's funny how I don't remember that exactly but it's bringing us closer now.

And then there's the fact that suddenly I'm having fun in the park again, a plot twist I didn't expect—I don't mean to suggest that it's always fun, like when some guy grabs my crotch first thing as I'm leaning towards him, so I duck under a tree to suck someone else's dick, and there's that horrible smell, but how do I stand up without being rude? He's pulling my hair, even though I just want to get away. I kiss him on the neck and say: I think I'm going to walk around.

So I'm on my way home, thinking how am I going to get that smell off me, or out of my nose, or wherever it's stored—I turn towards the statue just in case, and there's some short guy with a shaved head just standing there like my dream come true, I mean I don't have a type but if I do have a type then this is my type. I'm trying to decide if he's a straight guy imitating a gay guy imitating a straight guy, or just a gay guy imitating a straight guy, or something else, but we're walking over to the water tower, touching and talking a little, which is as intimate as it gets here, right?

We climb the hill and then I'm rubbing his head, kissing the liquor and cigarettes that taste so good because it's him, right here, up above which is kind of strange because then we can't help watching the cars down below and what does safety mean—I say there aren't as many mosquitoes out tonight, he says don't jinx it.

Even though I could rub his body and suck his dick all night long although how does his ass stay so tight, is he squeezing it the whole time, even though I'd be glad to suck every drop of spit and liquor and even cigarettes out of his mouth, even though I could pet him every day for the next year, he wants me to come. So I do. Even though I'm not ready. I'd rather piss instead and then start again but since this is what he wants it's still hot.

Living in a world of regulated narratives, we're all overcome by what we're most suspicious of, at least from time to time. I'm watching this gay couple looking at produce together—they're deciding on each item like it takes teamwork, and I want to be on their team. They don't know whether to get beets by the bunch, or in bulk. Can you eat the greens, one of them asks, and the other one says I don't know.

I say they taste kind of like chard—you can steam them or sauté them, or use them as a base in a vegetable stock. And they look over at me like I just interrupted their sacred space. The tall one pulls the shorter one closer to him, and the shorter one opens his eyes wider like excuse me? I just smile like I don't even notice they hate me. Remember when common wisdom told us marriage was on the way out? Then gay people stepped in.

I thought maybe it would be fun to get groceries, but now I'm stuck at self-checkout without any self except the one that doesn't want to be here. I don't know if there's enough space in the world for me to pretend there's space in the world. Sometimes I feel like a body drained of reason, and sometimes I feel like there's no reason for a body, and sometimes I feel like that reason.

Maybe I'll watch the construction site across the street again, how in spite of all these huge machines there's still so much human labor required, and somehow this feels comforting. But then there's a security guard looking up at me like I want to tear the building down. How does he know?

The main problem with community accountability is the community part. Exchanging one form of violence for another, here come the leaf blowers again. One day I'd like to have enough energy not to wonder if I have enough energy.

But then I'm in the park again, how did I even get here? Under the main cruising tree with twelve trunks, or that's what it looks like, although can a tree really have twelve trunks? I've counted, and there are twelve. In between the trunks I'm on my knees sucking this guy's dick, and suddenly everyone is around us—this group dynamic so rarely happens anymore, and what's even more rare is the way this guy holds my head to pay attention to me while he's also paying attention elsewhere, and this feels so good, my face buried between his legs as I feel something on my arm, yes, someone's coming, who's coming, and then just when I'm past dedication to this one particular task he says can I fuck you, and this is the best time yet, his arms all over my body, rubbing me into this world or out of this world and into another world.

And then afterwards we talk about the other guys, I ask who came on my arm, he says someone in a white T-shirt and black pants, Asianish, is this the language we use when language is spoken, someone's clothes and someone's potential race, but I guess I asked. Not that I've ever figured out exactly how to talk about race in the context of sex, I mean my tendency is to talk about the sex, what I'm feeling, what it makes me feel, and only race or anything else about the interaction if it comes up in a direct way. I mean here we are in what might be the most racially diverse sexual space in Seattle, so I'm having sex with so many different kinds of guys, that's just a given, but I don't want to establish some kind of catalog, do I?

Although then I always wonder if I'm making something invisible that shouldn't be.

I can tell this guy doesn't want to leave yet, even if he wants to leave—we've had sex in the park a few times before and it's always felt connected, but maybe not this connected. I think of giving him my number but does anyone ever call, so I just say we should do that again. He doesn't take the hint—even when it's this good it still stays here.

But back to the dance floor, the dance floor and sweat, sweat and my body without fear, walking out of the bar and I tell someone down the street that I like his green pants, turn around and smile as he tells someone on his phone that I just complimented him. He says it happens all the time, people stop me like this—he's joking. I say here's another one, and I blow him a kiss. This is why people drink, to get to this place, and I just need dancing.

Everyone's talking about the blue moon, but what is it? I mean besides a phrase, a phrase meaning never. When I was a kid, my parents went to a restaurant called the Blue Moon in the next town over from the beach town where we went on vacation. It was a cocktail bar, and my sister and I weren't allowed to go—it wasn't a place for kids, my father said—too many fairies.

But I'm realizing that my father's use of the word fairy to mean faggot, already dated when he used it, might now seem so quaint as to come across as sweet. Let me assure you that my father believed in neither sweetness nor magic. He needed to delineate the boundaries of my dreams. If my dreams were not his dreams, then they were not really dreams.

I wonder if my father used the word fairy instead of faggot because that way he could express his hatred more openly. Or if this was just the language of homophobia that he'd learned. Where does humor end, and violence begin? My father loved jokes, especially if you were the joke. This is how he would control you. You could laugh with him, and move the violence inside, or try to break the spell of his curse while everyone laughed at your lack of humor. Over time I learned that taking the violence inside was the only way out. What I mean is there was no way out.

Laughter can be a tool for many of us surviving violence, but it can also be a way that violence against us manifests. We all know that humor isn't really humor, if it isn't really humor, and still. I don't know how I ended up here, when I was talking about a blue moon. Maybe if I go outside, I can tell you.

Sometimes we need to hear what we already know, and sometimes we need to hear what we will never know. Sometimes we write what we need, and sometimes we still need. Do we write against trauma, or with it? Do we write in trauma, or out of it? I mean how do we write ourselves out of trauma?

The dream of urban living has always meant a density of experience, that random moment on the street that changes you. But now, when people say increasing the density, they mean building more luxury housing for new arrivals who only want an urban lifestyle with a walled-off suburban mentality—keep away difference, avoid unplanned interaction, don't talk to anyone on the street because this might be dangerous.

People talk about increasing this density as if it's a necessity for the future viability of Seattle. But viability for whom? If our cities are only destinations for the wealthy or soon-to-be-wealthy, what is the point?

How did the city become the environment of locked-in space instead of the place where all the locks are broken? I'm on my way to Pony, and some fag wearing a backwards floral baseball cap tries to give me the straight gay attitude for stretching on her building. Let me be clear here, I'm stretching on the railing for the unnecessary stairwell leading down to the entryway of a building called Onyx. There's nothing onyx—the building is gray, tan, and beige—it's like Florida meets the supermarket. But they do have that railing, which is useful for stretching my legs, especially since my usual place, the jungle gym at Cal Anderson, was filled with kids playing.

But I'm trying to tell you about dancing, yes, dancing— the point is all this jumping up and down—that's Thomas's style but also it's because he's a lot taller than me, which is unusual, and I want to get up to his eyes. There's so much joy in moving in and out of someone else's moving in and out—we're so close we could be touching, I mean we are touching, but it's only our breath. I didn't know I could have this much energy, sweat pouring down my face and I keep saying I'm going to stop, because I don't want to get too tired, but then I keep going.

Maybe the next day, and I'm walking to the park again, I mean it's night and I'm too tired to cruise but then I'm cruising and why, but then I hear something that sounds like a fiddle so I walk in that direction. It turns out the fiddler is packing up, but now someone's playing piano since there's one right here for Pianos in the Park. And watching the way the piano player moves is way more fun than watching the way the people cruising will never move me. Eventually it's just us—he's playing for me, and I'm dancing yes dancing—it's not like Pony, but still it's dancing. And then he's singing too—straight love songs, or straight not-quite-love songs, and I'm almost in love with him, especially when he stops, and says: I love that you're dancing.

Nothing about him leads me to believe he's not straight, except maybe the moment when he says why are you here? But I'm not sure I want to leave this moment to go to a moment that probably won't become a moment, so I stay.

When I moved back to Seattle three years ago, I wrote about my blue overcoat hanging on the knot of a tree in the park while I was getting fucked—cobalt blue, the color I saw for years on women's coats and then finally I got my own, found it at Goodwill in San Francisco and

I wasn't even looking for a coat, that's the best way. Actually I found it on the same day I found two others, all of them wool—the big puffy-shoulder magenta '80s one, and what was the other one? Oh, the long red coat that flares at the bottom like *The Sound of Music*.

The blue coat is the warmest, maybe even the warmest of all my coats—no, there's the large plaid one, but that's a men's coat so I don't like the cut as much except it's better for fitting more layers underneath. I got that coat when I lived in New York, and I'm pretty sure I didn't wear it once during the entire decade I lived in San Francisco afterwards, but good thing I saved it because it was definitely useful when it got really cold in Santa Fe—no matter how many times you tell people that Santa Fe is a four-season town, everyone still thinks it's always hot and dry, but sometimes in the winter the high would be 8 degrees and that's about 40 degrees colder than the coldest day in San Francisco, so I wore that plaid coat a lot.

It turns out I need that coat in Seattle too, even though the last time I lived here the warmest coat I had wasn't even that warm, but I guess I wore two sweaters underneath. When I moved back three years ago, I wrote about the rain yes the rain and how sometimes it's noon and you still feel like the sun hasn't come up, will it ever come up, will it? But at night, walking in the rain and oh the air is so fresh. Walking in the rain and there's no one or everyone and the trees yes the trees and how they get so tall, everywhere— something that would just be a little shrub somewhere else, towering to the sky between buildings.

It's raining today, but the sun will come back, it will come back because it's August—and I need at least two more months of sun, right? And those nights of wearing nothing but a tank top and shorts, and now you know I'm in the park again. I could tell you about the guy who says he's safe because he was married for 20 years and now his wife is going back to Mexico, but I say no, let's use a condom. And then he wants to take me to his mobile home on Queen Anne—are there really mobile homes on Queen Anne?

So he's fucking me under the main cruising tree, and I'm thinking about how this lack of pain still feels like a dream, a dream I barely imagined, and then I feel someone else's hands on my head, his knees right up against me, so I'm grabbing the back of his legs as he's getting harder and I think I'm probably going to regret it when I look up to see his face but then when I do it's porn when porn finally means something.

Walking back, there are people trying to get out of the tower—they got locked in, and one of them climbed the gate to get out, but the others are still stuck, their friend went to call the fire department. I yell do you need anything?

I don't know how to pick locks, and I don't have bolt cutters but they say thank you anyway, ask me my name, and then I realize I'm yelling right next to everyone else cruising like no one's stuck in any other way. Some guy comes over to me, and he's really tweaking—I say sorry, I just got fucked in the dirt. Then I'm walking down the hill and I think: Finally I'm ready to be a slut again. Maybe that sounds strange, because I've been a slut the whole time, but I'm ready to be a slut and feel it.

When people say something like oh the youth or oh the elders, I really just want to laugh because it's not like anybody's doing a good job of anything. I pass a neighbor on the street, and he turns abruptly to look at a cement wall. I'm always confused by anyone who says they're not depressed, but when someone says they've never been depressed, this is frightening. Apparently this shrub is known as America's Living Fence. Also, there's a dead fence behind it. But I love it when a bush grows big enough to cover a NO TRESPASSING sign.

It used to be that whenever I saw someone wearing sunglasses in the rain, I thought: What's up with that diva? But now I'm that diva, trying to avoid another migraine. I mean it's always there, but I'm trying to keep it in the background. Should I tell you it started when I went to a meeting for a new queer activist group, a meeting that promised a scent-free space, and when I got there I noticed a really strong paint smell. They said it was in the hallway, so we opened the windows and then there was a breeze blowing through so it felt better. But then the huge heating mechanism went on and made all this noise and someone closed the windows and then I could feel a headache starting but still I looked around at everyone else and thought oh, no one else seems bothered, so it must be all right, it's a scent-free space.

When was that meeting? A few year years ago, I think. And I've had this headache ever since. There's the trauma from the people trying to harm you, and then there's the trauma from the people trying to help.

It's a rare day of thunderstorms, and I've just walked an hour in the rain just to walk in the rain. Or just to walk. I mean I walk an hour every day, rain or shine it doesn't matter but today the rain is particularly dramatic. Up ahead there's someone wearing a tank top with the solar system on it, cute, and he gazes up at the house painted like a Buddhist temple, then steps up the stairs on the little building next door that I've always liked, four apartments with a doorway for each one right at the top of the stairs—kind of like a lot of buildings in San Francisco, I guess, but not a Victorian. Then he looks back, do I see his eyes yet? I mean how beautiful they are.

He says I like your coat.

I say I like your tank top, what's your name?

So I step up the stairs, and into casual conversation— do I kiss him hello right away, because of the way he's looking at me, yes, I think I do. He's visiting from Boston— he's lived in Seattle, and India, but he always ends up back in Boston. He's telling me this because I told him I don't like Boston. He likes the rain here right now, the thunder, it's so beautiful. That house, he says, I was looking at that house, and then I saw your coat, and will I see you again?

I can give you my number, I say, and he takes out his phone. It's a landline, I say—I got rid of my cellphone. That's great, he says.

I say we can make out now too, if you want, and that's when I'm kissing him, his phone is ringing and then my voicemail picks up and we're kind of laughing but still kissing after the phone hangs up and it's incredible the way we're both so present in the moment yes this moment—maybe this is what I've been working towards, to see the look in his eyes and to know that comfort. To go there, to allow it all to overtake me, to exist in my body, my body right now.

When I say that finally I'm ready to be a slut again, I mean I'm excited about sexual connection and its possibilities. The experience of desire in everyday interaction—wasn't there a time when my sexual practice matched my ideals, I mean my ideals for connection, and I'm ready to go back there. I've been ready for a while. But now I'm ready to make it happen.

When suddenly your tongue develops its own sense of space, the softness of this cheek, teeth another way to pull softness closer, why stop when there's no stopping no don't stop his hands on the back of my neck so tender I don't know if anyone has ever really described making out. I'm pushing him up against the wall yes the wall there are no walls except the ones that will support us. When we stop he looks me right in the eyes but we're so close I can't focus—I say you seem so present in your body, how do you stay so present?

What's important is that I'm saying what's in my head no I mean heart, yes I'm saying what's in my heart, and when I'm telling this story to Randy later he laughs at that part because that's what makes people nervous I mean it makes me nervous and that's where I need to go. Sleeping a lot, breathing, eating well—these are the things Charlie's telling me as we're making out, things I already do but even if we never see one another again this is perfect because I'm completely here. This isn't desire that just happens to me, it's desire that's an active choice. I can no longer handle the practice of promiscuity without the potential. I can no longer handle the separation of my life from my sex life.

When I say that finally I'm ready to be a slut again, I mean crossing the line between acceptability and an embodied truth. Refusing the boundaries of societal scripts—expressing desire as a form of accountability to myself. I'm ready for laughter to be part of my sex life. I'm ready for my sex life to be part of my laughter. I'm ready for my sex life to feel like life.

But maybe I shouldn't have said that even if I never saw Charlie again, our encounter on the stairs in the rain was perfect. I mean it was perfect, but it doesn't look like he's calling me back, so now it doesn't feel so perfect. Those 20 minutes of making out felt so complete, but couldn't he at least have called me back to say he didn't have time to meet again?

Voicemail is a form of relationship—so many people don't realize this anymore. I have entire relationships that exist because of voicemail. Like with Joey in New York—we rarely reach one another directly, but then we leave message after message, get cut off and call back again to leave more messages. It's almost like we're actually in conversation—every nuance and shift in intonation, the moments of excitement and heartbreak and exhilaration and breakdown and confusion and breakthrough—so when we finally end up talking, all the context is there.

When I say I wonder about marbles, I mean the pristine longing, the sparkle of light, the rolling away from darkness, the hiding in corners, the difficulty of carpet, the pounding inside the vacuum cleaner, the coolness in hands, the weight of forgetting, the jump of color, the texture without texture, the aim of emphasis, the bouncing against walls. As a kid, I collected marbles—this was so much better than losing everything, the way every day began and ended. But could I disappear, a marble rolling through a doorway used only by mice, bite-sized. Stare into the glory of this malachite green somehow sliced from a rock and shining in every direction.

Eventually all my marbles were gone. I don't know where they went. Actually, my mother still has a few of them in her living room, the prettiest ones, somehow on her display table, unable to escape.

But then Charlie's phone is ringing, and I can feel a clenching in my chest, or no, just below my chest, my stomach—and my heart is beating really fast—and then the voicemail answers, and I leave my message. It's a little messier than I wanted it to be, but I don't re-record it because it sounds vulnerable, and that's what I want, right? I don't just want to fling my hand to the side a little and think whatever, because I'm trying not to shut off like that. Then I hang up the phone, and I feel great, or maybe not great but calmer, more open, there's a softness in my chest.

Sometimes I look outside my apartment and see gay couples walking down the street and I'm filled with something that can only be called love yes love and I don't know what this means, since I can be fairly certain they don't love me back I mean I say this from 25 years as an avowedly queer person in the world, a faggot and a queen and whatever else, 25 years that these gay men have not loved me back so I can be fairly certain they never will, especially not in this town where most of them will not even meet my eyes they will not say hello they will not reply to a smile or a wave or a wayward glance, except with a glance in the opposite direction.

I know I live in Seattle. I know they call this the Seattle freeze. People say this is the Nordic heritage but it didn't even exist as a term a few decades ago. It's the way gentrification robs you of any perspective except the wrong one, this walking death, and Sarah Schulman says something in one of her books that really shocked me, something that I'm still getting over. She describes going to the LGBT Center in New York for a community meeting, and thinking: These are my people. Which is something I've literally never thought in my life.

So then I'm at Pony again. There's no smoke machine so I dance right away, but who are these shady queens? Queens, Joe keeps saying, queens, so at least I have that. Even though I thought his name was Nick but that's his ex-boyfriend's name, I met them at the same time. People are dancing, but they'll only dance with people they know. This one girl comes over to do a few moves with me, but then she literally says: I have to go back to my friends. Her friends are 5 feet away—why do people go to bars if they're only going to talk to the people they know?

On the way home, I stop in at the Cuff, even though I told myself I would never stop in there again. I'm at the urinal, and some guy tells me he's taking his t-shirt off and just leaving it there. He throws it on the floor and buttons his other shirt—finally, he says, I'm free of my girdle—thank you for talking to me, no one will talk to me because I'm 54.

And somehow this feels like the most connected moment of my night. I see a discarded Franzia box, and remember a former life. Really it was only a few months in 1997, carrying box wine around like it would save me.

Because of some guy I met at Basic Plumbing. He came home with me, and we took a shower together. He asked if he could wash my face—I'd never let anyone do that before. It felt so intimate. In the morning he left while I was still sleeping, or still in bed. He didn't even leave a note. That's how I ended up with Franzia.

An awakening, a shutting down. I'm in the herb store, wondering why they don't have what I came here for, and then I realize I can't remember what I came here for. Until I'm on the phone with Randy just losing my shit, I mean now it's the next night and I can't believe I live here. I mean I can't believe I'm trying so hard to have fags in my life, but nothing's working—none of these people who supposedly want to be friends can even commit to coming over for five minutes once a week.

Randy says it's not like it's better in San Francisco, and maybe he's right—last time I visited I was worried I might want to move back, but actually it just felt empty. Or not empty, but flat. Flattened. Like I was living a life I already knew, but there wasn't enough life. And where were all the trees?

Randy and I met at Blow Buddies. And look at us now, eight years later—I talk to Randy more than anyone in Seattle. Do you see what I mean about the phone? It's a life preserver.

There's a tree I love on the way to Volunteer Park, white flowers except in one tiny part by the trunk where purple flowers grow—every year this happens, or twice a year because in Seattle everything blooms twice, and I wish this wasn't just literal. I'm in the park—if I listen carefully enough, maybe the sound of the chirping birds will drown out the leaf blowers.

I wake up with a phrase in my head about trying to get my body back. Back from my father. Except I don't know if I've ever had it. Not in all the ways I need.

I wake up with a phrase that became a whole paragraph, but what was it? There was confidence there too, confidence that I would succeed. But then I'm outside, and already I'm too exhausted to reach down to pick up a good luck penny, what if I can't get back up off the ground?

I turn the radio on, and some soldier or former soldier is talking about watching pieces of his friend's skull blown off his head—I think there are limits to this kind of mourning. Then there's a thunderstorm. No, it's just the trucks hauling away the debris from the two beautiful houses they tore down yesterday. Making way for a new building to house people who could've been housed better and more cheaply in the old buildings.

Sometimes we wait so long that we're no longer waiting, and sometimes we wait so long that we're dead. Once I treated myself for parasites the way the doctors recommended, I treated myself and I never recovered from the treatment. Everyone says they want to catch up—I mean when they actually call me back. But I want relationships where we don't have to catch up. Sometimes I feel like an entire culture has misplaced something. And it's everything.

Suddenly I'm remembering a public conversation between two Great Straight White Male Writers. We've all made the mistake of going to this event at least once, right?

After Great Straight White Male Writer 1 reads, it's time for the Q&A. This is where we're supposed to find profound insight. The questions are always the same, so the answers can shine all the more brilliantly.

Great Straight White Male Writer 2 says to Great Straight White Male Writer 1: Who is your ideal audience?

And Great Straight White Male Writer 1 says: Everyone in my ideal audience is dead.

It's hard to imagine anything more damaging to literature than questions about audience. Then again, it's hard to imagine anything more damaging to literature than literature.

When people look at me with a mixture of horror and surprise, I think about the way the city of today is just a place for the gawkers to pretend they have a cosmopolitan outlook. Maybe it's a fashion thing, but it's also trauma. Can we ever separate fashion from trauma?

I thought I was going to walk through this cemetery, but instead I walk around the wall around the cemetery. So often there's more protection for the dead than for the living.

It's obvious that a gated community is a graveyard. A graveyard has gates, to protect the dead from the living. I'm worried that's what the city is becoming—suburban suspicion repackaged as imagination, consumption rebranded as creativity. Every new building looks like an office park, and we all know an office park is another kind of graveyard, walling off dreams in search of profit.

A graveyard can be a beautiful place to imagine the dead and our lives that remain, to study the stones and names and look at the way that tree pushes those graves to the side, another kind of history. A graveyard can be a respite from the living, even just to watch trees against sky, those clouds growing bolder. But we cannot live in a graveyard.

The dream of the city is that you will find everything and everyone you never imagined. Does this possibility even exist anymore?

I wonder what it feels like to be famous, says the ice cube. It means you never have any privacy, says the ice cube tray.

I don't really understand privacy, says the ice cube. I'm not sure how to respond to that, says the ice cube tray.

I just wish there was a solution to beauty, says the ice cube. Do you mean a solution for beauty, asks the ice cube tray.

I wish there weren't so many jokes about slipping, says the ice cube. Maybe a banana peel, I guess that one's okay. But when someone says you're on thin ice, it makes me feel like I'm never going to amount to anything.

I feel like we've been through this one before, says the ice cube tray.

That's easy for you to say, says the ice cube.

I'm just not offended as easily as you are, says the ice cube tray.

I'm not offended, says the ice cube. It's just that the whole world is telling me to click my heels together or snap my fingers or order something new from the menu or pick up the remote control or call room service or hide out in a fallout shelter or go on vacation or swallow a bunch of pills or go shopping for another pair of shoes or find a psychic healer or drown in my own sorrows. They might as well just cut the power cord.

Have you been crying, asks the ice cube tray. Something feels less solid.

It was just my insomnia, says the ice cube. I'm sorry if I woke you.

You didn't wake me, says the ice cube tray. I don't sleep as much as you think I do. I was just dozing off.

What's the difference between sleeping and dozing off, asks the ice cube.

Now that's better, says the ice cube tray. You sound like yourself again.

I worry about you sometimes, says the ice cube tray. I worry about you too, says the ice cube.

Well I guess as long as we're on the same page about this, says the ice cube tray, there's nothing wrong with a little worry.

But what about a lot of worry—sometimes I worry a lot, says the ice cube.

I know you do, says the ice cube tray.

I don't understand elections, says the ice cube. Who wins, and who loses—it doesn't seem to make a difference.

I'm with you on that one, says the ice cube tray. But what about the Supreme Court?

What about the Supreme Court, says the ice cube.

Those justices stay with us for a while, says the ice cube tray. Citizens United? I know we both agree on that one.

It just seems like no matter who's in power, there's always too much power, says the ice cube.

Oh, so now you're a poet, says the ice cube tray.

I'm bored, says the ice cube—is there anything good on TV? You know the answer to that question, says the ice cube tray.

Remember that art show we saw once, says the ice cube. Which one, says the ice cube tray.

It was about graffiti, says the ice cube. Oh yeah, says the ice cube tray, I remember that one. Banksy.

Basquiat, says the ice cube.

Shepard Fairey, says the ice cube tray.

Keith Haring, says the ice cube. Before he became famous. Like when the people are partying with the pyramids and fighting off spaceships and flailing in the streets and dancing on TV and the TV becomes the baby's head which is a baby on TV but the baby's still crawling through the end of the world so maybe we can find each other.

It's a little too obvious for me, says the ice cube tray. I like some of the lesser-known artists.

Like who, says the ice cube.

I can't remember their names, says the ice cube tray.

What about the one that tags KISS ME on the inside of the freezer, says the ice cube.

Now you're talking, says the ice cube tray.

I like political graffiti too, says the ice cube. NO MORE PRISONS.

That's just not practical, says the ice cube tray.

Everything doesn't have to be practical, says the ice cube.

The worst illusion of safety is safety—two UPS trucks, parked back to back, maybe someone will write a song about this. Whenever you think your memory is not as good as it used to be, it's important to remember there used to be less to remember. One problem with humans is the chain reaction of human thought. Maybe I mean action. One problem with human action is human thought.

I'm in a hotel that leads to a sex club, and I see this guy I've had sex with before, the curve of his back so smooth, a curve like comfort and can looking be the same as touching but then we're touching and it's so sweet. I reach for one of those new condoms, open it up and it's a peanut split in half—this is how dreams are made biodegradable, but then suddenly a group of straight guys arrives, maybe it's their party and we're not supposed to be doing this here, one of them throws me down on the floor with a huge pair of scissors in his hand, ready to cut off my desire and anything it might produce but then I twist his arms so far back the scissors drop to the floor. I use the scissors to cut the phone cables that are tying everyone up, but not the phone that will get us out of here.

Now the straight guys are gone. I look into a glass on an end table, and the liquid inside the glass asks: How can you justify your behavior? I say what do you mean, could there be anything more beautiful than our bodies together like this in the room? And the liquid in the glass is embarrassed—you're right, he says, and I look around the room to figure out how it can become a room again. Somewhere to hold us. How there can be enough room.

Adrian calls: Thanks for your message about my doctors' appointments—it felt so warm and supportive, and it reminded me that you're a consistently supportive person in my life, and I shouldn't fuck with that.

He wants to go back to our plan of meeting up once a week, at a specific time, like I originally suggested. I'm trying to feel like this is actually going to happen. How do you focus on a relationship if it never quite comes into focus?

Now that my view is gone, I can't stop staring at the black mold growing on the frame of the new building across the street—I'd love to take a workshop on crying, but I still haven't made it to a cuddle party. I'm thinking about the body as a potential, but a potential for what?

We make art from our neuroses, but do we make neuroses from our art? The transition from walling off desire to desiring walls. The way advertising collides with selfhood, and we all know who wins the lottery.

Sometimes the lack of critical engagement in worlds allegedly built around critical engagement stuns me—it stuns me. I can't tell if I'm hungry, or enraged. And what's the difference. I wonder if I'm the only person who still goes outside thinking something magnificent and unexpected might happen.

I walk towards the sun, stand at the bottom of the hill before the stairs to the street above the highway overlooking the skyline, and watch the shifting colors of the leaves blowing in the wind. Halfway down the stairs there's a friendly dog, almost too friendly because it keeps jumping up. I didn't realize English bulldogs actually jumped. But I liked English bulldogs even before I decided to like dogs, so it's okay. Also there's the sun, so this is a different world, flowers growing in a field which isn't really a field, just some rocks overlooking the highway.

I decide to walk up that grassy steep hill to help realign my feet so they don't hurt anymore, and when I get to the top I have to step over a railing to get back to the street. Then there are the usual gay couples who ignore me. Someone points in my direction, but actually he's pointing at a condo. I decide to go back up that hill again, so I go down a different way, and I notice someone else wearing purple pants, but actually I'm not wearing purple pants. She smiles at me, and then goes back to texting. There's that field of bluebells again, just past the hill I'm going to walk up, and when I look up at the window of a building that looks redone I see that someone is looking out but not out, and then halfway up the hill I realize it's not as pretty this time. Maybe it's not as pretty because I'm already thinking about writing about it.

Halfway up or maybe two-thirds of the way the grass turns to mud and moss and then just mud and cigarette butts, and I keep almost stepping in dog shit. Back on the street, I'm walking up the hill that usually seems overwhelming but now it doesn't, except that now the sun isn't out anymore and I'm cold. Suddenly I'm sad too, and when I get back to my block there's some really loud noise, maybe the construction is going on late tonight. Actually it's someone with a leaf blower, blowing allergies right into my face, and now my head hurts. There's a container of dental floss on a chair in the lobby of my building, I do need floss but I don't think I want someone else's.

Maybe there's nothing straighter than a gay sex club. I walk into the video room, and there are five guys on the bench, naked except for towels around their waists, acting like they're just hanging out. They even have those trauma-tized I'm-a-dude-but-I'm-turned-on expressions. I want to yell girls, this is a sex club—you can have sex in here. But I'm here too, silenced by the dehumanization of complicity. Three of them leave, I sit down. Then I say why is every-one acting like they're straight? The other two guys leave without even looking at me. This is only the beginning.

The difference between satire and what's going on in the world is that the goal of satire is to illuminate hypocrisy. I walk by a boarded-up house, and there's a real estate sign that says EXCLUSIVE. Why is it that a little depression goes a long way, but a lot of depression goes nowhere? The balance between something that's too awful to comment on, and something that's too awful not to comment on. An update from the yoga boutique: nuclear-sunset-pattern hotpants made of recycled plastic bottles—the tag says "Dreaming in the clouds, and loving the earth."

One problem with the human interest story is that so often it doesn't seem interested, or humane—I mean mobilizing a personal narrative in service of a humanizing agenda is dehumanizing. The only thing worse than a baby boutique is a dog boutique. The only thing worse than a dog boutique is a dog spa.

Realism is overrated, but just because something is overrated doesn't mean it shouldn't be realistic. The good thing about falling in love with a phrase is that it will not love you back I mean leave you. But doesn't it seem vaguely pornographic when someone you've never seen before opens his cellphone charger port to ask if you have one like it?

Walking through the back side of the city, under the highway and then next to it, watching the views go by—there's one up ahead, oh, thorns. The Amazon towers and the underbrush. An almost-shack next to a '60s apartment building next to condos next to a fence next to another highway entrance next to the clouds. As long as the contrasts last there might still be hope.

I take off my scarf, coat, mittens, sweater, shirt, tank top, shoes, and socks, and then I dance right there on the cement. I dance for the sun on my skin, for the way my body suddenly feels alive, for the way I need this in spite of the glances from the few people around. Who don't want me around. I dance for them anyway.

But I don't want to get too tired, so I put my clothes back on, and walk uphill as it starts to rain. And I remember how the rain clears my head. There are three figs that have fallen from a tree, or maybe not figs but something like figs. The first one I roll down the hill for fearlessness, and it takes off. The second one I roll down the hill for staying present in my body no matter what, and it rolls away quickly, between the wheels of a car and still downhill. The third one is for letting go of the relationships I don't need anymore, and of course that one gets stuck.

I'm trying not to write about how Adrian keeps letting me down, because everyone keeps letting me down, but then I run into him on the way back from the park—I actually thought I was going to run into him, but then I didn't, and then I did. I kind of just feel distant, making small talk, when really I just want to say you don't want a real relationship, right? Eventually I say you haven't called me. He says it's because I can't think of a time when we can hang out. I say you can call me anyway. At the end I give him a hug and it feels like a real hug, I mean he's letting his whole body go so it feels like we're closer. Are we closer?

At Pony, I'm back to taking photo booth pictures of myself—they have a new pattern on the wall, which is white rectangles inside black squares on a white background, and it's incredible. Now we have the straight couples so drunk they're in the gay bar with cocks on the wall, talking to me. They love my photo booth pictures, so I love these straight couples, in the way that love can be transitory and conditional. Also, one of the guys is hot, something about the bow tie and gray shirt, curly hair a refuge for thought. From thought.

I don't know if I'm the one that convinces them to do a photo shoot that starts with cocksucking, but I know

I'm the one that says I need to see the results. Then I'm at a table with people who work at the thrift store, they're talking about someone who came in to buy a Halloween costume for her kid, and she said: I want to dress her like an Indian princess.

In second grade, I dressed as a Mexican for Halloween— I think this just meant wearing a poncho my grandmother bought for me. I never liked dressing up because I didn't want anyone to look at me in that way, but I did like candy. I don't think anyone understood my costume, and I don't know if this means they were less in league with white supremacy, or more.

In third grade, my whole homeroom class went to a place called Turkey Run Farm, where we lived like Pilgrims for three days. We dressed entirely in undyed burlap, slept on hay in log cabins or in tents, ate from a root cellar, and used a latrine.

I went to a school that prided itself on being the first integrated school in Washington, DC. I don't remember learning that colonialism was an honorable path, and yet I have this anecdote to prove it. I remember each of us had to make our own pocket out of burlap that we would tie around our waist, just like the colonists had to do. I was so proud of my pocket, which I decorated with lace that I'd sewn on myself, an elegant accessory, but my teacher tore it out of my hand, and said "a big tsk and a boo for you," because no male colonist would ever wear a pocket like that, and she handed me a plain one to replace it.

My favorite way to die is to stay alive as long as possible. You know that moment when your hair suddenly looks perfect, but you know that as soon as you step outside it'll be ruined so maybe you never go outside again. Sometimes I think the language of rights is the language of blight. A headline about J.Crew, but I read Jim Crow. Is there a synonym for a synonym? One is uniform, and the other is the uniform.

When a movie quotes other movies in order to make a movie about movies that's really about walking: "Did you report your purse stolen from a dog," quoted from *Dragnet*, in *Los Angeles Plays Itself*, which reminds me of Jafar Panahi's *Taxi*, where two people meet in a taxi in Tehran, and one of them says "What's your specialty?"

"Mugging." Then there's Nina Simone in *What Happened, Miss Simone*, where she says "I'll tell you what freedom means to me NO FEAR." Or I'm sitting in the booth by the video clips at Pony, trying to decode them, but now it's just one woman with a perm, singing in a variety of campy eighties outfits. The movie that isn't really a movie, and the movie that is. Maybe if the sound was on, I would know what she was singing, but I'm having such a good time, it's like I'm escaping into myself. Also, I'm escaping.

Even though no one will dance with me, I know it's going well when someone asks me if I'll give the birthday boy a lap dance. It's a group of Black and Latino fags who kind of remind me of New York—dressed conservative but total queens. I say I don't give lap dances, but I can give you a kiss. But now the smoke machine is on—it's amazing how much that horrible device can terrorize me, leaving my head in hollowed-out pain for days.

I'm outside dancing with Free, the doorman, and he asks me if I'll dance naked and covered in fake blood on a rooftop for his movie, I guess I would be a vampire. No, dancing isn't the word, is it? Rolling around and eating each other's flesh.

Free says I want to see your, what's the word?

Sass, I say.

Sass, he agrees.

But horror is not my place of worship. I want to map the place where self-hatred intersects with internalized oppression. Repression. Self-expression. Depression. I'm getting ready to cross the street, and a car pulls over, blocking the crosswalk. Welcome, I say grandly, and twirl around, welcome to the crosswalk.

Four women get out, they want to know where the Madison Pub is. I say I'll take you there. One of them hands me a mini bottle of liquor, and I don't tell her I haven't had a drink in over a decade. I just say no thanks. They pull me into the bar, and I think okay, just for a minute. I don't know why I thought they were straight at first, just that I didn't think lesbians went to the Madison Pub. Or maybe it was the straight couples from before.

I haven't been to the Madison Pub since I worked for Friend to Friend, so I guess that means almost 2 decades. I still can't believe I can say something like that now.

Anyway, it's packed. I guess it's a sports bar? These gays look at me like a spectacle, but they aren't unfriendly. One of them is touching my thigh, he says it's because he likes my pants but he leaves his hand there and I'm ready for more so then I talk to him and his boyfriend for an hour—there's some kind of flirtation going on, but the more they talk the less I like them, and I can tell this is going to take a lot more talking, so I go home, and read about the David Wojnarowicz show at the new Whitney Museum, which literally sits on the ground where Wojnarowicz once cruised for sex and sensibility. Simultaneously I feel disgust, and a craving.

When I first discovered Wojnarowicz's work it was right after his death of AIDS in 1992—I was 19, escaping childhood and everything I was supposed to be, gasping and grasping at the possibilities of living fully in a world I knew wanted me to die or disappear. Reading Wojnarowicz I immediately felt my rage and desire in print for the first time. Lust and loss as a part of everyday experience—the way it's everything at once, you don't get to choose unless you choose everything.

Nostalgia increases with each misrepresentation, marking the death of the imagination, increasing misrepresentation, but what about when it's a nostalgia for death? Museums filled with the nostalgia of the gentrifiers: remember when death was all we had—oh, those were the days. Is there a difference between nostalgia and gentrification, or are they two elements of the same process of cultural erasure?

The key to gentrification is more gentrification, every cultural institution in downtown New York fighting to own what they displace. I remember the Wojnarowicz retrospective at the New Museum in 1998—I was so excited to finally see this work that had meant so much to me, the actual work, not just photocopies on my walls. But walking around that show, all I could think was that he was dead, and the work in this context was dead too.

In one of the Wojnarowicz gallery shows accompanying the New Museum exhibit there was actually a beautiful piece rolled up on the table, grenades and burning houses—I had never seen that one before, and it felt like everything I had ever wanted. I signaled Andy to distract the only person working, but he didn't catch on.

And then I went to look at Wojnarowicz's diaries in a cloistered New York University library. You could only gain entrance if you proved yourself a scholar—they gave me white gloves to look at the diaries, and I thought about ripping a few pages out. I imagined Wojnarowicz would have wanted me to do that, but I got too paranoid about owning a stolen commodity that would surely increase in value with every exhibit, each new book of reminiscences that I crave in spite of all my critiques.

But Wojnarowicz was part of the art world, and his rage was a commodity the art world consumed. The angry artist smashing out the walls at a gallery that showed his work—even if the gallery deserved it, what a clichéd sort of masculinist triumph. If he had lived, would he have unlearned this?

Nostalgia for the pre-gentrified time or place or space might be one of the worst forms of gentrification. If there always was a better time, nothing really matters now—we can never re-create what we never really created. The most successful museums are not just coffins for the dead, but coffins for the living.

Have I ever been to a show at a museum that truly moved me, that's what I'm wondering. Once, I realize. Nan Goldin's *I'll Be Your Mirror*, which starts out in black-and-white like it's so long ago, but it's just the 1970s, all these gorgeous queens posing for the camera, lesbians and fags with long hair, transfeminine makeup shots invoking and satirizing Boston's frigid pose. Everyone is walking into tomorrow, suddenly so bright with the saturation of color and then we're in New York.

Nan Goldin follows her friends and lovers through drugs and violence and dreams and drama, a quarter-century of drama, all the failure and success, the taxi rides and bars and broken beds, her eyes bruised and bloody after her lover beats her up, somewhere near the middle of the show, and then everyone is dying.

Wait.

Everyone is dying.

I cried so hard at that show, cried even when I was trying not to cry, cried even around all those people, although not as much as I would have done without all those people—I went back, back to cry again, and do you know what, that show was at the Whitney. I'm crying right now, just thinking about it, how AIDS and drug addiction and suicide transformed all our lives I mean I was entering the world as an avowedly queer person right in the middle of it, with no other context.

I'm thinking about a phrase Martin Duberman uses in the introduction to *Hold Tight Gently*, his biography of Michael Callen and Essex Hemphill, two more brilliant gay artists who died of AIDS in the 1990s. He writes about gay men who have *physically survived* the AIDS epidemic.

After blowing the leaves into the street, and then out of the street, and then into the street, and then out again, this guy takes out a rake. He actually has a rake. And then, once he's done, he takes out the leaf blower again. But when did love become privatized? When did lust become loss? Do you want some food, this guy asks me, assuming that I would only be dressed like this if I were homeless. Or maybe it's because I'm trying to exist in public space? Even when people in Seattle are nice, they're not nice.

I don't know the difference anymore between desire and loneliness. I just know that when I go in the hallway at Steamworks to stretch by leaning against the wall in all different shapes, dancing to the music so my body is the wall I mean my body is open, there's no one here to open with me. When I leave I just feel gross, like my desire gets me nowhere but inside the machine I already hate.

Maybe it makes sense that I'm thinking about David Wojnarowicz as my hope for the communal possibilities of desire in everyday experience dwindles into loss. For the last month, every time I go to the park I have sex that I regret afterwards. Last night I wondered why I couldn't stay hard I mean even though I already knew it was because no one really touches. And I guess that's why getting fucked in the park can feel so transcendent— the intensity of the physical experience overrides the lack of connection.

Sometimes there are moments to hold onto—going to the park during the day with Gabe in the fall chill, but then it's not chilly anymore, so I take off my layers, and then I decide to lie in the grass, even though maybe it's muddy, and Gabe rests his head on my chest while I angle my hat to protect my face from the light. Then, when I sit up, Gabe's telling me about a game he used to play as a kid, where you write something with your finger on someone's back, and they have to guess what it is.

Let's play, I say, let's play, and then I'm doing that thing where I kind of hum like a little kid, I mean it's a laugh no not a laugh but a gentle sound of pleasure that means I'm here, all of me, and that's why Adrian is kind of laughing when we're kicking pinecones, I mean he kicks a pinecone to me because he knows I love kicking them, and then there's that humming like I'm a little kid, and I'm free. Finally free. I'm free.

Alyssa calls one day and says she's right around the corner, should she come over for a few minutes, just to say hi? She remembers how I've been working so hard to have this with Adrian. How she and I used to get together every week, but now she doesn't want that, is it her new relationship or her job or something else I will probably never know. Why did we spend all that time getting so close, I will always be wondering. But then she comes up, and says oh, that color on you, it really makes your eyes pop. You look so huggable.

And then, when Adrian calls, just to say hi, and keep me posted about things, which is something he never does I mean he's doing it now and that's when I think something's working. Matthew calls—we've been trying to hang out, but it hasn't happened yet, except for Anastacia's performance, where are you now? He's at the Pine Box with Cassidy. So I go right over there, even though I don't have any energy at all, but then the sun comes out and everything is gorgeous and I go inside and it's fun just laughing with them while they're drunk, watching the waiter who's incredibly hot drink three shots before work and oh, he keeps looking at me, but he's not our waiter.

He makes some grandiose gesture with his hands, and that's when I know he's a fag, and Cassidy says I could've told you that right away. Matthew wants me to give the waiter my number, but we haven't even talked. And then it turns out Gabe's obsessed with buying a condo, even though he doesn't have the money for the down payment. And I guess I do have the money, but I can't get a mortgage. So we go to open houses, one of my guilty pleasures no longer guilty—Gabe's snapping photos of these places where we'll never live, a gorgeous one that's way too small, but in my ideal building, and then a rundown one on the top floor of an ugly building that's cheap, and by the highway.

That dynamic between trying to decide whether you hate the city where you live and wondering if you can buy a condo must be what they mean when they say the American dream. Gabe tells me about being part of a gay rowing club for years—oh, it's because we run into one of the guys from the club at that second open house, with his boyfriend or someone that looks like a boyfriend but I guess I shouldn't assume because here I am with Gabe and what do we look like? Anyway, Gabe says I tried so hard to be a part of the club, but in the end no one really cared about me at all—but it was my fault, because I should have realized that earlier—these A-gays, I was never going to be a part of it. And I say it wasn't your fault, it was their fault for being so tired.

And then I call Gabe when I get home, and he says was that okay? I say yeah, it was great, and he says because you know how I get insecure—but I called you. I say yeah, that was perfect, you called me just as I was thinking of calling you, but I didn't know if I had enough energy.

I was thinking about that rowing club, I say—all those horrible people who couldn't appreciate your beauty. And Gabe says thank you for saying such nice things. And I feel like maybe I can have the relationships I need.

There are two different kinds of dancing—the kind that's good exercise, but not good exercise for the part of my heart that isn't just a pump, and then the kind that's emotion through motion, a flight into presence—yes this is what it means to really let go to hold on to never let go to go on. And then one of the bartenders comes out to introduce himself, he says I love your dancing. Really, I say, because sometimes I'm the only one dancing for like an hour and I feel kind of strange. He says I love that. We hug, and then he's touching me on the chest, and we're dancing for a few moments before he goes back behind the bar. I always see him smiling in my direction, but before I was worried he was laughing at me—do you see how words can help?

One of my favorite things about bars is how people are always touching you. It's the way alcohol opens up the pathway between felt sense and spoken, and somehow it took me over a decade of not drinking to appreciate the lowering of inhibitions that meets the way I want to be anyway, or gets closer. Except when it gets messy—the trembling of addiction, the plunge toward a stumbling self, the annihilating beauty, the annihilating beauty of what, the way he touches me so easily and I'm touched.

This sentence for his tongue in my mouth, for the corner at the Eagle where he's sucking my dick and suddenly everything feels so easy. This sentence for when he needs to smoke and you know I'm not going out there, but then I realize it's really inside, inside my head already because the smoking area is a covered patio with an open window that goes right into the bar but still I'm waiting for him to come back. This sentence for his shame, that's what it is, even though he brought me to that corner the first and the second time around, that's why he keeps leaving and pretending that nothing's going on.

I should've left right when he said he likes Bangkok days and Berlin nights—or when I told him I grew up in DC but I hated it, and he said I've been all over the world, I've been to every city that's worth anything in this country, and DC is dirty. Even though I'm pretty sure that in a different context he would say he's dirty, right, that's how these fags are, but then he was touching me and I couldn't help thinking about how much I need this touch.

But what is the point of connection if it's so disconnected? I won't pretend that I don't go home and go online, even though it's way after I should be in bed or maybe not way after, but at least an hour, I won't pretend that I didn't already post an ad on craigslist but no one responded because I said I wanted to make out, except now someone has responded, and he's cute, so I won't pretend that I don't try to hook up except he's in Federal Way so that's not going to happen, but I won't pretend that I don't call the free phone sex line in San Francisco because I need the charge of someone else to get off, and I won't pretend that's not weird, maybe something to work on, but first I need to work on this, and I won't pretend that I don't finally talk to someone who sounds like a mess, but I don't realize how much of a mess, until he says: I dropped a fucking cigarette I can't find it. And then the line goes dead.

But before all this, when I'm still at the bar, I'm so present. Did you see the way I just approached this other guy right after, approached him because I can see something in his eyes that I love, approached him without fear. I mean something felt hopeful, even with all that smoke. Even if it should've ended before it started, right from the first snotty soulless bragging, or at least with the overt racism of his DC is dirty comment, but then he was kissing me. Just like that.

Like that night when this whole exploration of trying to figure out a sex life that matters, when it started with another bar, another bar and another hookup with someone really tired but hot, another hookup that hit a dead-end so fast but remember, there was an emotional opening, right?

I go back to the voicemail that I left Joey, that Joey sent to me and I saved it so I can listen to it now: I feel like I'm going to cry and I'm back in my body and I'm shut down. Partially it's that it's too toxic to be there, how hurt people are, how sad, is it weird to say that? And also how much it means to me to connect with these people anyway, even when it's not but maybe is also intimate.

Even when it's not but maybe is also intimate.

Even when it's not.

But maybe is.

Also.

Intimate.

When someone talks about a sense of time, I wonder if there's sense in time. A gap in reason. A reason for the gap. How do you write what you really feel without feeling what you really want? I mean I've never lived somewhere for so long, and still not felt like it's home—is this what it means to get older? Yoga boutique update: gray spider web capri hotpants. These pants come with a red tag pledging a donation of $1 to the spider web of your choice.

Wait, where did that spider go? I was just about to catch it, so I could set it free. I mean set it free, but not in my apartment. Sometimes I stare at a sentence to see if it's alive. If I can't sense a sentence then maybe there's no sense. When I say a sentence, I mean a thought. When I say a thought, I mean a feeling.

When Patti Smith says Robert Mapplethorpe elevated his subject to the level of art, I know what she really thinks of the subject. How long has he been dead, and still she's uncomfortable with his sex life.

This is the photographer who made dicks in chains into high art—where does she think his inspiration came from?

I didn't know about Smith's connection with Mapplethorpe until she wrote about their friendship in *Just Kids*—filtered through Patti Smith's romantic gauze, what cannot attain delusional grandeur? Maybe that's why now, several years later, people still talk about that book with almost universal reverence. The book where Smith uses Mapplethorpe's wild gay sexuality as a foil to her straightness, his ruthlessness in pursuing fame as a way to naturalize her talent, his brutal death of AIDS as a way to make her a fuller person.

And now she wants to talk about what Mapplethorpe sacrificed for artistic success, but not who he sacrificed. Who she sacrificed. Instead she talks about singing Christmas songs for the Pope.

Why is it that whenever I feel better, I can remember feeling worse, but when I feel worse, I wonder whether I actually felt better? There should be another word for this, this exhaustion, except I don't want to know it because I don't ever want to feel this way again. Maybe there's a word for this feeling of not wanting to know the word for the other feeling.

When people stare at me like I'm doing something horribly wrong, just because I'm doing something a tiny bit out of the ordinary. For example, I'm leaning against a tree, to relax my back. I know the tree doesn't mind. Why does this person?

Sometimes you think you've solved the problem of representation, but really you're just representing the problem. The same gay men who worship at the throne of straight masculinity, who denigrate femininity and anything associated with it, who write Straight-acting or Sorry no femmes in hookup profiles, these same gay men are now expressing shock and outrage that their neighborhoods, including the one where I now live, have become hot destinations for hordes of drunk straight homophobes.

When these upstanding gay men were busy pushing out anyone not wealthy or white enough for their fine manners, everything was fabulous, but now that they're the ones displaced there's a problem. I'm sick of hearing about the mythical neighborhood where everyone belonged—they could have helped to create that neighborhood, but instead they created this.

When you wake up smelling burning metal, hoping you didn't leave the stove on, and you realize that's just the smell of a thousand leaf blowers. What do we call the type of gentrification where a place looks more and more like a city, and feels more and more like a fence?

There's a rusty nail in my bathroom sink—is this a marriage proposal?

I'm still holding out for the day when we can all marry corporations.

When I open a book all the way to its binding and see there are actually stitches, this gives me pleasure, but also I know that the commodification of creativity is a dead-end. And it doesn't have to be this dead.

I'm inside, and I'm out. I'm inside-out. But then a trans woman on the street stops me to say I love your style, honey, and I start crying. I'm walking back uphill, and some fag I've seen around says hey girl!

Why can't it always be like this?

Movement across borders, movement of borders, movement without borders—remember when this was the dream of the city? Once I kept a poinsettia alive until summer. I think I was 12. The leaves kept falling off, but I didn't want to believe in death. This must have been when I would change the words of sad songs to make them happy—soon positive thinking would give way to positive drinking.

Not that I didn't enjoy singing "I think I'm gonna live and be happy-ee-ee" in the shower, hoping my father wasn't going to unlock the bathroom door with scissors again. As if singing could shield me. As if imagined joy could become joy. As if a shield would have helped anyway.

I'm not sure why so many anti-rape advocates still insist on saying that rape isn't about sex. It's as if sex is supposed to be this pure thing, but how often does anyone really experience this? The way language fails you. The way language fails. The way language fails to protect.

What does nothing feel like? Much worse than nothing. But then I'm dancing, and nothing matters. No: everything matters, because I'm dancing. I mean what matters is I'm dancing.

Still nobody's joining me, but when they play "White Horse" I'm giving some crazed runway all the way to the door and almost outside, then turning around and flinging my body in the air with abandon that isn't only abandon I mean now I have more control when I fall, rolling on the floor because I'm trying to go all the way down to the ground when I need to, yelling all the words, and then later, when I'm outside again, and Free wants me to teach him how to fall, so we're falling together. And I feel like I'm ready to live here. I mean I feel like I'm living here. I mean I feel like I'm living.

Remembering incorrectly is the greatest art. Remembering correctly is why people are tortured. Making art can be torture, but the torture of art is not the greatest art. The greatest art of torture is not to be tortured. But at what cost?

The best way to avoid bad sex is to search for good sex online, until you can't find anything but the searching. Confession: sometimes I boil water, but then I can't remember what it's for, so I let it cool down, and then I boil it again. The failure of writing to do anything but write, and can this be its potential?

The most expensive art is a sense of belonging. The best way to remember a sense of belonging is to remember incorrectly. The correct memory is a memory of nothing. Nothing costs more than nothing. Remembering nothing costs more than remembering.

When someone says enjoy this little bit of sun we're having, but actually it's already raining. To trust someone so untrustworthy. And this is what we're told is love. To fall in love with this trust.

It's been a year since I found Adrian at Pony—or he found me—should we celebrate by going to Pony, or somewhere else? And what does it meant to celebrate, anyway? I've never really figured this out.

We're standing on that part of Olive Way that slopes downtown, this view just like the view when I would step outside of my apartment at Faneuil Hall in 1996, and then sometimes I would walk by Magdalena's, after she moved into the Sealth Vista, and she would be leaning out the window, waving hi with Katie when they were getting messy or just acting messy and we could all be messy together. All the apartment building names in Seattle that don't quite make sense, and maybe that's one of the only things about Seattle that makes sense.

And that's where the internet café was—I'm telling Adrian, the first time I ever went on the internet—I didn't really know what the point was, and Andy had to convince me. Adrian loves to talk about the past, to hear about the past, to think about the past, and suddenly I feel like maybe I actually have a history here, even if it's from so long ago—1996 was 19 years ago, no wonder it feels like it's not connected to my life now, when I've been here for 4 years, but still I don't feel a sense of place. I feel like I could leave tomorrow, and I wouldn't even care.

How do I bring the sense of place I felt here almost 20 years ago into the present day—I mean a sense of belonging. Is that even possible? When Gabe gets to my house he's so excited, there's all this excitement, I wonder if we're dating. I mean I know we're not dating, but I wonder if we should be dating. Obviously I don't know how to date, but he's always dating someone—I can't believe how many relationships he's had, one after the other. He says: Maybe I would be happier if I focused on something else.

Bathrooms at art museums, what could be more romantic? Gabe says he's finally realized that he doesn't want to be with his first boyfriend anymore. We're watching a video where the artist says he lets his assistants be creative, they can paint the sculptures however they want. But of course they don't get any credit.

Gabe says he's tried for so long to conform, but all that does is get him to the same place of failure. I guess I can't really ask him for dating advice—too much trying to be the other person, getting pushed away for not being the other person, getting pushed. I just wish I wasn't so lonely.

Then Andy and I are talking about the internet café, how Andy dragged me there to go online, but I wasn't sure whether I wanted to be online. Andy says you were there because I wanted to look up gay skinheads on the internet, it was just something social, a social way to be antisocial—in the beginning it was more social than antisocial, because it was too expensive to be online for too long.

And the end? We're living it now.

There are two times in my life when I felt like I had a home, and unfortunately they were both in San Francisco. There is memory, and then there is the memory of memory, and then there is the memory of something not-quite-memory, and this is maybe how dreams work. I miss all those faggots I once knew, who always thought that masculinity was the worst thing. I do mean the worst.

My mother calls to tell me about *Spotlight*, a movie about sexual abuse by Catholic priests—she says I think you recommended it to me. But I've never even heard of it. Of course, my father was a priest I mean psychiatrist who sexually abused me. One advantage psychiatrists have over priests: access to drugs to use on their children I mean patients. One disadvantage: lack of access to God. Anyway, when I tell my mother about her Freudian slip, she says: I can see how you might think that. Which would be a great title for a movie about psychiatrists who sexually abuse their kids.

Sometimes it's hard to write about the saddest thing in the world, I mean someone else's saddest thing—you witness too much or all at once I mean so early, so soon in a relationship the breaking down the flooding the collapse the holding onto what will never work, but holding on anyway. I mean a relationship with someone else's pain. His relationship with someone who will never work.

How do you tell him to get out of the relationship, when he already knows, but can't. I mean how do you tell him if he's already telling himself, again and again and you watch, you say it too, again and again, and again and again he's back in the same relationship.

I would like to say that this is why I avoid these kinds of relationships, but actually I just can't figure out how to start them, how to open up from the comfort of friendship into whatever that other thing is. The comfort of desire? The comfort of desire met. I worry that won't happen for me here. I worry that if I move somewhere else there will just be another here.

Short story: Last night you gave me a candy cane. I took it because you were sad. Even though I don't eat candy. Today I'm sad too.

Love story: I pick up the new Patti Smith book, read a few sentences, and drop it back onto the table. The woman next to me looks over. I hate her work, I say, it's so overwrought. Me too, this woman says.

The problem with words is that they are only words. And then you forget them anyway. The problem with forgetting words is that then you use the wrong language. The problem with the wrong language is that then there are no words. If we were all stuck without words then there would be more language.

Who decided that language would be permanent? I'm searching for a way out, which is also a way in.

Gabe doesn't want me to write about him, so is this sentence already a betrayal? But if I'm trying to create a world for myself with other people, how can I avoid writing about other people? I mean how can I write without writing about people I might love. I call my grandmother, who's in the hospital, and she says: I still don't know what it was I mean I guess it was my heart.

Some guy stops his bike in the middle of the street while heading down a steep hill with cars behind him, and says hi, I'm on a scavenger hunt—I'm the leader, I'm putting a crossword puzzle in a novel, do you know where Top Pot Donuts is? Yes, I say, and point him that way. What book is it? Something Russian that I found, he says, and veers in the wrong direction before turning left, so his bike doesn't slip downhill. No one honks. This is a Seattle where I can actually dream.

One problem with depression is you lose context. One problem with losing context is you get depressed. Sometimes it's easy to forget that desire brings me into a sense of self, it's the world and its lack of options that shuts me down. The dream of presence is no longer present.

When you're writing about the mundane details of your life, it's important to write everything down in the moment. Because after the moment passes it just feels too mundane. I know I get energy from spending time with people I care about, but why is it so hard to find these people? As soon as I see Adrian, my energy picks up three levels. The first level is not feeling so alone. The second level is feeling happy to be with this person. The third level is the connection we create.

But then we're walking in the park and I'm not so sure of our connection, I mean Adrian feels so distant. I ask him what he's feeling, and he says he's trying to notice everything that's going on around him, which is what I'm trying to notice too—the wind through the trees and the way that whenever you look up, there's always a different frame between branches and sky. And all that air in between.

Stopping here to close our eyes, the light with our eyes closed, the wind on skin and through clothing, the sound of the rain, what moves and what doesn't, is there a vibration inside, and what does it connect to, now moving slower through the dirt and the sound of our feet in the gravel, leaving behind what we don't need, and when we get to the stairwell looking out into the light, the light of another city, the city, this city, that sparkle up ahead through the trees, light through our bodies, leaving behind everything that's weighing us down and when we walk down the stairs it's all gone, right, let it go, it's gone.

And how when we walk home through the streets of houses now, and then businesses, and then apartment buildings, something's calmer, the way inside can change outside, and Adrian says I feel so much better. This is love, I think, as we hug goodbye. This is presence.

And now Brian and I have a way of making plans that works, I mean after we go on our walks together, walks different than the ones with Adrian, I mean we talk so much, but somehow it doesn't feel exhausting because there's a charge. A charge that feels energizing, but also calming. And also we're on a walk to the park so I can lean against trees when I need to, which is really the best way for me to hang out with anyone. The charge is through our words bouncing into one another because Brian likes to ask questions about everything, it's an intellectual connection but also our bodies. And there's a sweetness. We're almost exactly the same age, and even though we've had totally different experiences it's fun to have that really direct generational link. And then all the differences because Brian grew up in a small town, and he's been in a relationship for 16 years, and they were monogamous until a few years ago, and we've never lived in the same cities until now.

I don't know where this is going, but I know it's going somewhere—this time Brian says what are you doing this weekend, before I even think of saying let's make a plan, another plan, since if we do it by phone it takes Brian two months to actually commit. This weekend? That's in two days. And now we're hanging out in three. This is what I want, relationships that go somewhere, that connect, that have a through-line.

At Steamworks, it turns out that you win a prize if you can guess how many keychains are in the container behind the glass. But why keychains? You're so cute, this guy says, before running away from me. I go into a booth with someone who was looking at me before like I was out of his league, I mean I don't know it's that guy until I get inside the booth and then I just see his cock pointing upwards and I'm on my knees. Did I mention that I finally figured out a way to have condoms at all times, after 20 years of going to these places? I just put a few condoms and some lube packets in a little plastic bag, and then I attach the bag to the inside of my towel with safety pins. I don't know why I never thought of this before.

I think the key is to have sex with the guys who look at me like I'm unattainable, I mean go up to the ones that I crave too, but sometimes they can be so distant, even when they're present, and that isn't the kind of connection that will leave me laughing my head off in the hallway like now, I mean I feel so good that I know I should leave, but actually I feel so good that I can't leave. Besides, this is the music I live for, the hard building layered house and, yes, there's a DJ now, and I'm dancing in the hall again, and you won't believe this, but someone actually stops to dance with me, this Black queen who seconds ago was giving masculinity forever—now she's holding me tight and we're queening it up and this has never happened before, in all the times I've gone to sex clubs and danced, finally, we're here together, twirling in the hall until we twirl apart but yes, I'm still twirling.

Someone's watching me dance, I mean someone who looks curious and turned on, instead of the usual, and when I stop he says why are you here, instead of at a dance club, and I say because I can't deal with smoke machines, and now he's rubbing my chest, and it feels so sensual. I close my eyes, his hands all over my body this feels so good I mean I could stand here all night just like this, but then I pull him up and say let's go somewhere, so we're in the cubby that's next door to the one where I was before—I wanted to make sure it wasn't the same cubby because I spilled too much lube on the floor, it got pretty slippery.

The best thing about sex is when it opens you up to the possibility of more sex. After the shower I still feel great, even though it's two hours past when I should have left. But I still want to dance, so even after I'm dressed and wearing too much clothing I'm throwing down a little bit of bathroom mania in the mirrors, kick the legs up in the air while leaning back into the sink, and when I'm checking out downstairs the clerk says we were watching you on the video cameras because we got the message that someone was dancing in the shower, and girl, you were really working those moves.

And then even when I get outside I still feel good. How is it in there, someone asks me—is it just old people? He's kind of cute, and since he's asking me this question I figure he thinks I'm kind of cute too—if it wasn't so late, I would grab him and start making out. I'm laughing and saying tonight I actually had a great time, I mean I don't always have a great time but tonight I really did. And then I turn the corner, and these really young queens are complimenting me on my coat. We're from West Seattle, they say, like West Seattle isn't just a neighborhood in Seattle. But also I'm thinking about how racially diverse West Seattle must be, if all these queens grew up there.

They want to know how I got such a classy name— where are you off to? One of them is taking a video of me, saying this is Mattilda, and then I'm twirling for the camera and posing with the other queens. I can't believe there's a line around the block for R Place, but don't even ask me to describe the crowd—I have to cross the street just to get away from all the cologne. And then on

Boylston I'm stretching on that railing behind some condos, and the queens coming from C.C. Attle's are looking at me from the distance, like oh no, trouble, so I yell girls, don't worry, I'm just stretching, and one of them says it's like God put it there just for you. And then another one wants me to point my toes. And I'm wondering why we can't always talk to one another. Then right before my building there's a straight couple giving me shade about my outfit—Amelia Earhart, what are you doing out tonight, the guy yells.

And I say honey, I'm flying.

You know when you think something might be happening, but you're not sure, so you get that clenching in your chest that's your nerves, and that wired feeling in your head that's desire? And then you realize it is happening, and there's just that wired feeling. I mean I could tell he was following me through the park, but I wasn't sure why until he pulled out his dick on a stairway in broad daylight, or the closest it gets to broad daylight with low clouds spitting drizzle like we're still living in a rain forest, but anyway within seconds I was on my knees.

Now we're on our way to somewhere more private, and I feel so calm. But the truth is there aren't really any private spaces in the park during the day, they've all been trimmed back to prevent a dream of connection from breaking through everyday exhaustion. He's excited too, I can tell, as we're walking down the open path, and there's a huge shaggy dog up ahead—look at that cute dog, he says, and goes over to pet it, although it turns out the dog is too shy.

I like that this guy's personality isn't swallowed by silence, and he seems to know where to go. We choose the closest thing to a place where people can't see, and then yes I'm on my knees again, trusting that he's watching out for both of us, my craving for words long past, my mouth past language and into another language, the thickness of desire feeding me, the taste of my spit on his skin, the taste of his skin, the feeling of his hand on the back of my head. And I place my hand over his, so he'll keep it there and then he's pumping, yes, he's pumping, yes, please, and then there it is, the moan and the shuddering until he pulls away.

That was amazing, I say—if you ever want to do that again, I live right nearby.

And he surprises me by saying really? That would be great.

So I give him my number. He says he can't give me his because he's married, it has to be really discreet. I say I don't have anyone to tell, and then we're walking in the same direction. I'm wondering if I think he's cute, are those little blue plugs in his ears or headphones? And when he goes up the hill to retrieve his bike, I wonder if he just left it there, leaning against that tree.

He surprises me by calling right when I get home. He says I'd definitely like to do this on a regular basis if you're into it—I work downtown on Mondays, Wednesdays and Fridays. And I say Wednesdays are the best, and Fridays can sometimes work, but call anytime, it's just me here, leave me any message you want. He says okay, I'll leave you a dirty message. And I wonder if this is really going to happen.

What do you do when there's a beautiful area of flowers and tall grasses where yesterday someone was living, and now it's set off by a rope with a sign that says WARNING: NOXIOUS WEED TREATMENT ZONE? A jury of your peers. A jury of your peers. A jury of your peers. Has this ever happened?

I'm lying in the park even though it's cold and a little damp but there's a sun break and I love the feeling of sinking into the grass, the air blowing all over, this is the only thing I ever want to do, ever again. But what's that noise over my head, it sounds like 1000 dragonflies, is that a drone? Don't be ridiculous, I don't even know what a drone sounds like.

I take off my hat and eye mask to look up—sure enough, this guy is flying some miniature aircraft, in circles over my head. I put the eye mask back on. This is all I have—this sun, a little bit of joy in the park, the air. Why does this guy think he can ruin everything, just to play with his expensive toy?

The problem with good dreams is when you wake up. You stare across the street at someone staring in but it's a vase. The music is saying house music will never die, so you turn it off. There's nothing like the policing of language to make you speechless. From childlike excitement to overwhelming sadness so fast, and which one is more like childhood. When you're walking down the street, and you think you see JoAnne, but then you realize no, JoAnne's dead, but still you think maybe. So you look this person in the eyes, just in case, and she doesn't know what you're looking for.

Everybody knows about glass houses, but what about glass shoes? That feeling of dissociation when you realize you just listened to a whole program on how to get Democrats elected. The question is always who will kill for this country, rather than will this country ever stop destroying the world.

One problem with the war mentality is when there is no war. Another is when there is no peace. Translation assistance: when someone says "I don't hate anyone," this means they hate everyone. If knowledge is power, why does it always seem like the people with the most power are the ones who reject knowledge?

I swear I just saw a dog-walking jogger pick up a piece of dog shit with a plastic bag and then throw it back and forth with his friend a few times. Of course one of them was wearing an I Love New York T-shirt. Calling for unity is one of the most sinister ways of silencing dissent.

Seattle is the fastest-growing big city in the country, so of course all the wrong things are growing the fastest. When someone says don't take it personally, I feel like they're telling me not to be a person. They say we're on the same side, and then they fight for the kill. They fight to kill you with every word. This is education. They say let me speak, and really they mean let me silence you. This is gentrification. Now you can rent a boutiquement at the Lexicon.

People who talk about being on the wrong side of history like that's a bad thing must not have read a lot of history. The disappearance of voice in service of objectivity or science or literature, a fully-made bed as the symbol of righteous indignation I mean proper décor. The worst response is no response. Whenever I hear about helping people out of the shadows, I wonder about helping people to stay in the shadows if they want to.

You'd think they would have fixed the pavement before installing those rainbow crosswalks, but I guess the cracks make everything more realistic. Each rainbow crosswalk cost $6000, so you know they used good paint. And one of the crosswalks leads right to the police station. An imagined community is one way to describe heartbreak.

But why is there such a close relationship between thinking you're about to have a breakthrough, and thinking you'll never be able to break through? I'm pretty sure well-placed hatred can heal as much as undeserving love, and it doesn't hurt so much to let it go. I look out my window, and there are three Mormons talking to someone who's nodding off. Is this a comedy routine? One of the Mormons blushes every time he looks up at me. Maybe he thinks I'm in Heaven.

But finally everything is solved—there's a new building called Identity. Actually, there are two buildings called Identity, just down the street from one another. But how do you know which Identity is the right fit?

It's a Wednesday, and the guy from the park actually calls, says he's had a few beers and he's nearby, am I available at noon? Sure, I say, and then he calls again at 11:30, literally just as I'm getting out of the shower, rushing to pick up the phone and he says I'm right down the street, is it too early—I can wait.

I'm worried that I can wait means he can't wait, so I say no problem, as long as you don't mind that I'm still kind of wet, and then he rings my buzzer just as I'm putting clothes on, just in case he's the kind of straight guy that doesn't want to see me naked, and when I answer the door I can tell right away that he's smashed.

11 a.m. is a little early to be smashed, but I'll take this girl in whatever way she wants to show up. This time he surprises me by taking off all his clothes and lying back on the bed. His body's really hot, sinewy and smooth, lots of tattoos, nipple piercings, he really does have the whole bike messenger look. At one point he's practically whining, which is kind of funny for a straight guy, telling me to grab his balls hard, pull his nipples. Follow the fly, he keeps saying, although I'm not sure what he means. He's panting and grabbing his dick and pushing my head up against his balls and after he comes I kiss his thighs really gently, rub his chest and he lies there for a while and I think this is the best part, I mean I was getting a bit worn out before, but now I feel so calm.

He starts telling me about his brother who got an online degree from Cambridge and now he's in business school, he's so proud of his brother, and I wonder if Cambridge really gives out online degrees. He says: and here I am, working at DoorDash—sorry, I'm really ADD. And I wonder if he's a tweaker. He does have a crease in his cheeks that might be from gritting his teeth, and I can't tell how old he is but maybe about my age.

Call anytime, I say—you don't want me to call you, right? No, he says, I have to be really careful. But you can always say no.

Suddenly I'm remembering a housemate interview at a collective macrobiotic house in Boston in 1995. The person in charge decided to show me how they cleaned their scallions before cooking them—the inside of every scallion must be free of all dirt, he said. For some reason I applied for that apartment anyway. I didn't get it. Needless to say, I have never cleaned the inside of a scallion.

I remember when I used a rubber stamp to mark STOLEN on all my money, and sometimes businesses wouldn't take it. Irony is only dead if you insist on killing it. One day there will be an art installation where someone sits in a room answering phone calls, and everyone looks in and says really? No, really. I'm in that room already. What's it called when you can't decide on the right music, so you listen to the sound of the water flowing into the measuring cup?

Unfortunately most people only believe in two kinds of history—the history that never was, and the history that will never be. I'm reading a glowing cover story about a new arts organization that throws events in buildings soon to be demolished, and it's all about love, I read, over and over again, it's about love and love and love and love, and when I get to the end I find out that the founder's motto is Collaboration with Gentrification. Sometimes the violence of people allegedly trying to help is the worst kind of violence.

I'm getting depressed by all the simplistic things people are saying about depression right now. When a celebrity dies, people want to help you with your depression. The rest of the time: no big deal. No one ever talks about the structural reasons. Look around. Are you depressed yet? If not, something might be wrong.

One good thing about Seattle is that people on the street are so unfriendly that when someone smiles and says hello in a genuine way it's like your whole life just changed. My mother calls to tell me about watching soccer—she says they're crying and embracing and touching each other on the face and you don't see that kind of affection between men, I don't see that.

Unfortunately I don't see that either. When someone says dogs are like people, I worry about dogs. The best thing about a rhetorical question is the answer. Walking outside, I try not to look at the dead bird on the sidewalk. Then it flies away.

The guy from the park calls again, even after I miss his call, and he sounds excited when I answer. Are you free, he says, I just got off work, and I'm about to grab a beer at Citi Market. Definitely, I say, I just missed your call by like a second, and he laughs.

I throw the bedspread over my sheets, and put on my favorite LCD Soundsystem, the one that's just titled by the number of minutes you get, or I think that's what the title means, but isn't it longer than 45 minutes and 33 seconds, and when I look out my window I see him biking past my building, maybe looking for the best place for his bike I'm guessing, but then it's been a few minutes so I wonder if he's making another DoorDash delivery. Oh, here he is.

When I open the door I realize I do think he's cute, really cute with those dark beady eyes and the way his tight lycra bike shirt emphasizes his big curly hair when he takes his helmet off. Do you mind if I sit down and drink a beer first, he says, and I laugh. He says or I can wait. I say yeah, let's wait, and I rub his back, I feel excited in almost a childlike way—this is what sex can give me.

The way his breathing is stop all the way and then start again, my desire and his, there's so much to feel I want to stay here in this feeling, stop all the way and then start, and he leans back onto the bed like last time but this time he's not all messy, just leaning back to savor everything, letting me take charge, my hands rubbing his body, his balls, his thighs until he's kind of whining but this time it's softer, yes, he's saying, yes, I'm coming, and there it is in the back of my throat again, my hands up to his chest until his dick starts to go soft, then kissing the edges of his pubic bone until I rest my head in the cleft of his pelvis. This is the best time yet, so sweet and sensual.

Now he's getting dressed. He says: I took a week off because my back was hurting, I'm doing this DoorDash thing to recover from rotator cuff surgery—it sure as hell is cheaper than physical therapy, and I make money. Hurts like fucking hell, though, but I figure it has to get worse before it gets better, right? I'm just waiting for my shoulder to heal so my friend can tattoo over the scar, it's only a few inches but still.

I say well anytime you want to relax, feel free to call. You said Wednesdays are best, he says—right? And I think it's sweet that he remembers. I'm rubbing his back again, and I can't tell if this makes him nervous.

Down the street, there are three tough guys with leaf blowers, hosing out dead leaves from underneath the ivy. The militarization of landscaping must end. Also, the landscaping of militarism. I thought maybe this new building was designed for mass suicide, but it turns out they're putting balconies in where those glass doors are. I'm worried that in order to have the kinds of relationships I want, I'll be forced to have the kind of relationships I don't believe in.

Some people are afraid of roaches, and some people are afraid of rats—I don't think it's like are you a dog or a cat person, not exactly. I remember when I lived with both, in San Francisco—I would reach to get something out of a cabinet, and a few roaches would come tumbling down—no big deal, right? A big deal was if I left even a scrap of food out, and then there would be hundreds of roaches all over the counter. Or, every morning when I turned the light on. I got used to it. But then there were the rats, which ate the roaches, and that was nice for a few days until I came home one night, and there was a rat in the hallway, scurrying away from me until it got to my doorway, and then it slid right under like it was home.

Everyone knows rats are shameless, but what does this say about shame? The worst part was when I looked outside one night into the shell of the demolished building next door, and there were rats so huge they looked as big as cats. I lived on the top floor, which was great because I was a late-night person and I didn't want upstairs neighbors waking me up in the morning, but then the pigeons lived in my ceiling, and the rats would chase them, or they would chase one another, and sometimes something would die, and I would hear it scratching in the walls, so sad, this was what really terrified me. But I lived in that apartment for six years, and I think I loved it—not the roaches or the rats of the pigeons, but something about the expansiveness of my life anyway.

Before that I lived in a commercial loft in New York, where we never saw a single roach and maybe that should have been a sign that we were being poisoned. We lived above a lampshade factory, across the street from an electrical power station, I wore bracelets made of pipe clamps, and I had my mercury fillings removed—these are some of the things I remember when I think about how the chronic pain overwhelm started. Or, it was always there, it got worse, it's still here. And the New York City pollution—mind, body, everything in between. That's how it felt then, in the late-'90s. I hated living in New York, but the last time I visited I thought of moving back. Sometimes I'm not at a loss for words, but this doesn't mean I'm not experiencing loss.

Walking down a block just up the hill that I guess I've never been on before, a beautiful block with lots of trees and colorful houses and a really interesting Art Deco apartment building tucked into a driveway—and newer buildings too, but newer buildings with beautiful trees, and I discover a tree with a mystery fruit I've never smelled before. So I sit on the newly constructed steps of a house that will surely be torn down soon, I mean it's a nice house but it looks abandoned, and abandoned in this neighborhood only means one thing.

Sometimes the same walk can be an obstacle course, an amusement park, and the first time you ever looked at a flower. I'm trying to decide whether I've ever felt a burst of energy that isn't delusional. And then I get so tired that I feel like I'll never feel anything else except this feeling, this happens every day. When you wake up from a dream where you're driving on a major street in the city where you grew up, but when you look at the street sign it says Hobo Street. This is after I look out the window in a friend's apartment, and see she's right in the middle of a huge river leading out to mountains, how much is her rent? I'm trying to get out of a cab but it turns onto the highway where there's no road, just a foot or two of snow streaming out into the future.

What's it called when you keep finding yourself looking into parked cars to see if that's a headrest or a person? This song is saying meet me on the dance floor at midnight, but midnight's too late for me now. So this song is telling me to say that you'll be mine until the end of time—I've never believed in the mine part but the end of time, oh how that always ends faster than I thought. There's a tiny green worm crawling up the orange wall in my kitchen, and I wonder if I can get it to do that all the time.

When you grow up in the dominant colonial power in the world, maybe it's impossible not to sometimes find yourself thinking colonial thoughts. Sensing dissent as a form of consent, is this a question or an answer—I mean how can I be singing along to a song glorifying permanent ownership of someone else's desire as the definition of love?

Here's my guide to electronic music: Is there a vocal, and does it ruin everything? Someone is trying to teach a child to walk in the right direction, and the child isn't interested. I'm rooting for the child.

But I think I found the best way to dance at Pony—walk uphill in the pouring rain with seven people of different genders, ages, personal histories, sensibilities, and styles, seven people who say they want to dance, and it's a Wednesday, when there's no DJ, but also that means there's no smoke machine. And then we get there, and everyone's actually dancing, and dancing differently, each of us throwing down our own special moves, but also throwing them down together, and the bartender even changes the music from the doom-gloom they were playing to something way dancier, nothing I recognize but everything has beats, different kinds of beats but still beats and this is incredible, I mean I hope we can do this every week.

Every Wednesday at 8, I'm asking, and everyone's saying yes, and when the video switches from sixties camp to seventies porn I get that feeling like I just want everyone to touch me at once, and then when I'm getting tired, or no, after I'm tired but when I'm really tired, they throw on LCD Soundsystem and I'm singing along to the drumbeats, falling onto the floor, I mean falling and rolling and jumping up to fall again and when I leave it's 10 and the rain is softer, and I stop to look at a fluorescent light in the doorway of a white Victorian that will probably be torn down soon to make way for more luxury apartments, but right now that light is the most beautiful thing I've ever seen.

The best dancing is always a fall from grace. I mean the most graceful fall. I can't remember why the naturopath told me to rub sesame oil all over my body, but it feels so soothing. I love it when I run out of something, but I already have a replacement. So maybe I'm saying I love it when I don't run out of something.

This woman at the farmer's market picks up a particularly gorgeous bunch of beets, holds it up to me and says: Do you think these are in season? Meanwhile, at the café down the street, they're having an art exhibit of pillowcases with huge glittery eyes sewn on top. He's a real people person, this guy says to me, about his dog. I was just thinking that pragmatism might kill me, and then I looked it up in the dictionary. Maybe I'm already dead.

When my straight boyfriend comes over again, I'm expecting the usual, whatever the usual is, but then as soon as he gets in the door he's grabbing my dick. Wait, what's going on? He's drunk again, that I can tell—he rips off his clothes and lies back on the bed for a second but then starts pulling my clothes off too, and then he twists me around so he's leaning on my belly to prevent me from reaching his dick, while reaching for mine, sucking it really softly, mostly at the head, which feels pretty good except for his scratchy stubble, and then he starts playing with my ass too much, and then I just feel exhausted, even while I'm sucking his dick, I mean even though there's more passion, like he grabs my head and we're making out, he pushes my hands to his neck. But it's his passion. And I'm just going along.

Afterwards, he says: It's so nice to have a lover. I kiss his neck, and pet his head. This is so sweet, in a way, but also so confusing.

While he's getting dressed, he starts telling me his life story. I have a 17-year-old at home, he says, and it's so hard—I'm just waiting til she turns 18 so we can figure out what we're going to do. January 21—I'm counting down the days. I met my wife 18 years ago, and I was going to drag shows then—one night, some friends came over and said do you want to dress up with us and make some cash, and then they brought over all these clothes and I was like wait, these are women's clothes.

The money was pretty good—100 dollars, and we would split it three ways. A year of that, and then I'm thinking wait a minute, there are a lot of hot guys around. Now I'm doing DoorDash to save money and go back to school. I used to be in the union, 22 to 25 an hour or 30 if I was the foreman, and at DoorDash I can make 30 an hour so it's a pretty good deal. I used to be in the union, but I can't do that anymore, going to go back to school, maybe become a radiologist, then you're basically a doctor and you have something to retire on. I'm only 40 now, but I have to think about my future.

Just when I think this might become be a regular thing, he stops calling—maybe he's shown me too much, that's what I figure. Then one day I step outside and there he is, riding by on his bike. I don't know whether he sees me, but I know he doesn't stop. Suddenly I feel like I've lost something.

The best thing about Seattle is that people walk around in the pouring rain like nothing's happening. I mean Adrian and I are walking around in the pouring rain, and he says going to Graham's improv comedy shows is one of the only times when he sees Graham so happy. Like when I see you dancing, he says, and he says it so casually that I know it must be true.

We want things to happen in the expected way, and when they don't happen in that way we drown ourselves in expectation, or the lack. Or, we know nothing will ever happen in the expected way, and so we drown ourselves. And when we try to pull ourselves out of this expectation, when we try to create something else, we fail, and then we're back to this expectation.

When I say we drown ourselves, I mean we suffocate. There is no water. If there was water, there would be a bridge, and if there was a bridge, we might take it. But a bridge is a balancing act. A balancing act is still an act. An act is not the same thing as feeling.

I'm saying there's a point when we give up, I mean we give up and keep going. We ask ourselves: Is this worse than drowning? We drink eight glasses of water a day. Some of us drink eight glasses of water as soon as we get up in the morning, just so we don't feel thirsty. But there's always a thirst.

And yet, sometimes there's light in dark rooms. We all know this. This doesn't mean we should stay in the dark. I'm at Steamworks again, and when the DJ comes on the sound system is suddenly four times louder, and that bass is my heart. That bass, and these showers where the water is always hot, and the pressure strong enough to make relaxation intense. Even after I've given up on these places, given up so many times, but still I'm back, and I'm lying on a bed in one of these rooms with a guy I'm not entirely attracted to, but it's so sweet anyway, the feeling of his hands rubbing my body, the feeling of his hands rubbing my body while he's fucking me, the feeling that I finally figured out how to get fucked and feel relaxed, feel relaxed the whole time, or almost the whole time, even when I sit on this other guy's dick that's kind of too large, and I can tell he's used to people having trouble by how he says are you okay? But it doesn't hurt at all. Maybe this isn't what I thought I was looking for, how to get fucked by random people in a softer way, but still it feels beautiful. It feels like there can be light in these dark rooms, a lightness in my body, and maybe I can bring this into other rooms.

But then sometimes the shower is not enough. Even if it's a great shower.

How is it possible that these guys who go to sex clubs all the time have never figured out how to have sex? Or, have only figured out how to have sex in this way that means more shutting off than opening. I keep saying I'm learning to find what I need in the places that will never give me what I really need, but does this just create more need?

How can I ever wash off all the shame and disembodiment in this space where we've all come together to touch, that's what I'm wondering now. The glorification of free will as a deadening of heart. There's nothing like a song that says I FEEL LOVE over and over to make you feel lonely.

It really did look innocuous. Just an envelope with one sheet of paper inside, why this sheet? I assumed it would only be the usual rent receipt, but actually it says my rent is going up $500 in two months. That's 40 percent—my rent is going up 40 percent in two months. When I'm actually starting to feel settled here. Is it better for your rent to go up $500 when you love where you're living, or when you hate it, I don't know.

Now I understand why everyone in my building has been leaving. This is what's happening to each of us, one by one. Seattle is a boom town. The Capitol Hill light rail stop just opened—the anticipation was already fueling displacement, but now it's in overdrive. My rent has gone up 70 percent in four years.

The state of real estate. The real estate state. The state of the real. I ask the building manager what she thinks, and she says: I feel like I'm working for the devil.

When I was a kid, I loved looking at the real estate listings. I fantasized about a bigger house, one more elegant or modern, one without problems. Maybe a house where I could have my own entrance, my own escape.

My grandmother was a realtor, the one who's still alive, and I always liked her apartment too, because it was an apartment in the city. It felt more sophisticated to live that way, around other people. Other people who weren't just the people holding you hostage.

I fantasized about living on the top floor of one of the new condo towers that started appearing across from car dealer shops and strip malls in the suburb where I grew up, but in a different part, the part that was becoming something else, I wasn't sure what. Maybe then I could look down on everything. Maybe then I could escape.

I don't believe in real estate, but I don't believe in not believing enough to not believe. I know that I don't have what I need in terms of relationships, in terms of the queer dreams I once thought would hold me. And so I fantasize about this other kind of stability.

I fantasize about having my own laundry machines. New machines. Machines that have never been used by anyone else. So the residue of other people's detergents and fabric softeners doesn't wake me up in a haze of toxicity in the middle of the night. Every night. And if it's not directly on my sheets then it's pouring into my windows from the pipes downstairs. So when I walk into an open house for a condo, and I see there's laundry in the unit, it gets me high just to touch all that smooth metal, open up the door and imagine.

Then there's the smoke. Someone's always smoking outside, and it always comes in my window, because I live upstairs from the entrance. And then I feel like I'm suffocating in my own apartment. The only place where I can really relax. Except that I can't relax.

One fantasy about real estate is the fantasy of control. That's the fantasy I'm drawn toward now, now when I realize my rent has gotten so high that I could pay the same amount, and have a mortgage. I could pay the same amount, and have my own laundry. I could pay the same amount, and live farther from people smoking outside. I have the money for the down payment. I just don't know if I can get a mortgage. I mean I already applied for preapproval, just to see what was possible, and they turned me down.

How do we start this conversation, my mother and I? She's promising that she'll help me. She says her promises are good—well not always, she says—I know I've promised you things I haven't followed through on. But I want to follow through this time. I'm laughing, and she says don't get hysterical.

That's what my father would always say when he succeeded at getting her angry—Carla, don't get hysterical. The psychiatrist was diagnosing the problem.

I'm struck by the way language becomes embedded— my mother isn't saying I'm the problem, but still she's using the words he used to silence her.

There's a lot I don't remember, my mother says, and she's telling me again how after my father died she asked his therapist if she would tell her some things, and the therapist said I know this might sound old-fashioned, but I still believe in keeping his confidence. And I know I'm moving into the place in this conversation where I become my mother's therapist, this conversation that started when I asked my mother for help.

My mother wants to know why my father was always so angry at her, she wants his therapist to solve this. But he was angry at everyone, everyone in the family. That was his problem, not yours, I tell my mother.

But he was the one who liked to have fun, my mother says—I never wanted to have fun with you.

I don't say what I should say. What I've already said. What I've said so many times. How many times can I ask my mother to acknowledge what she will never acknowledge?

I say don't compare yourself to him and decide he was the better parent. I'm thinking about the last time my mother visited, and she told me that she looked to me for support when I was a little kid. Because she knew that I saw, she knew that I saw what was going on in their relationship. She saw it in my eyes.

I wanted to save her. Because she would never save me.

What am I trying to save her from now?

I haven't driven a car in at least 15 years, but somehow I still wake up from dreams where the brakes don't work. This time I fly diagonally out the window and land softly underneath a lamp post while the car I was driving stops just before hitting me, but usually I'm about to tumble off a cliff in one of the cars I drove as a teenager and it's the fear that wakes me.

When I first learned how to drive, of course I drove as fast as I could, over 85 on the highway in a car with a speedometer that only went to 85, a Volvo, safety for the upper-middle-class teenager. The whole car would shake while I was singing along to "Magic Carpet Ride." We're all stereotypes at some point, right?

But how did this plant overflow, I must have given it too much water. Wait, there's water pouring down from the light fixture. I stand on a chair to figure this out, and I see there's a tiny sprinkler inside the light—I don't remember noticing that before, how do I turn it off? And then I realize I'm dreaming again, wake up into a day that doesn't feel like a day, not anymore, just something already crushed. A car is not a magic carpet, but still.

Before I wake up, I'm wondering if the landlord installed that sprinkler to get me to move out. All the discarded stoves and refrigerators in the basement hallway that have been there for months, appliances for the broken heart. It's amazing how hard it is to get someone to make out at a sex club. It literally takes hours. When I say make out, I don't mean it as a euphemism for something else. I mean lips to lips until there's no space between desire and possibility.

I wake up, and listen to the Violent Femmes. For the first time in years—the first album, of course. I still know all the words—or, not all the words, but enough to start a cover band called Nonviolent Femmes. We'll sing Violent Femmes songs at sex clubs until everyone leaves—this is what it means to love art.

Yoga boutique update: Rorschach test hotpants. Splatter-paint Jackson Pollock, recent murder, or field of flowers? $76. But do the Rorschach test hotpants go with the yoga shamrock sweatshirt, price unknown? That's your second Rorschach test.

How the familiar can be so jarring. How the familiar can be the worst sense of displacement. Sometimes I think desire is the same thing as being haunted. And sometimes I think desire is freedom from pain. And sometimes I think desire is temporary amnesia

There are eight cops across the street to handcuff a woman who's not resisting. Four police SUVs. Now there are 11 cops. I think she's being arrested for screaming.

Gabe isn't calling me back. He told me to keep calling, since he doesn't have voicemail. He says he never calls, because he's too shy—but then we were on a roll because he was calling me back. How many times do I call, until he answers? Desperate times call for desperate acts, but what if these acts only make me feel more desperate? There is hope without walls, but there are so many walls.

We collapse against our limitations, creating more limitations. Is it better just to collapse?

When did I start relying on unreliable people? I don't want to say when I started relying on people. Apparently the party for my 25-year high school reunion is called GOOD VIBRATIONS. Maybe when I'm up against this tree in the park, and then when this guy is done another guy walks by, after I'm hugging the first one goodbye, and he says what are you up to. I say I'm waiting for you to fuck me. And he already has a condom on his dick when I'm sucking it—I'm thinking that one surprise effect of PrEP is that the closeted types in the park are now more likely to use condoms than before. Especially Black guys—I know there's that stereotype that Black guys don't use condoms—I don't think that was ever true, but it's certainly not true now.

Anyway, this guy is fucking me and it's even better than the last time he fucked me, maybe because I'm already relaxed, resting against a tree with bark so soft it almost feels like cork and sensing into the way my whole body can vibrate from inside, and then when I'm walking home all the gas comes out as I'm heading downhill, and I hope this means the bloating in my intestines will go away too.

My high school reunion is at someone's house that's barely two miles from our school. I can't believe anyone would choose to live that close to that time. Maybe there are two kinds of people—the ones who found high school traumatizing, and the ones who aren't really people.

So someone created an email list of everyone in my graduating class, and sent this to us, this notice about GOOD VIBRATIONS. I guess there were only 95 people in our class. Already I'm reminded of names I'd forgotten— I'm trying to decide whether to send an email to this list, asking if anyone wants to arrange a conference call to chat about what it was like to be queer at our school. Trying to decide whether this would be horrifying, or productive. The fear that I'm suddenly feeling makes me think it would be productive. My breath getting stuck somewhere between pelvis and chest, a clenching in my throat. A jitteriness followed closely by exhaustion.

No, it's right in the center of my intestines, the part that's stuck. I mean the part that's stuck all the time, the part that woke up in spasm just today, that throws off any possibility of internal balance reaching external calm. How everything is related, even when it's not related.

Even just to send the email. Even just to say maybe we could chat about some of the things we were too afraid to say then. Even just to mention the stranglehold of liberal homophobia.

I wonder what these people remember. It took me 25 years to be curious. So I send the email, and I feel something between elation and calm. An expansion in my chest. If this is all I get, I'll take it.

Sometimes I go to Steamworks just to feel like I have something to do. I know the difference between feeling desire, and wanting to feel desire, but the feeling part only lasts so long, and then I'm left wanting. I guess it's the same thing with the park, although in the park there's beauty regardless—if I can't find those arms then at least I can find a nice tree trunk.

It's amazing that I was just thinking how homophobic my whole grade school experience was, and now I hear that someone is teaching one of my books there—and, they had no idea that I ever went near that school. If the high school that once forced teachers to stay closeted can now be teaching my work, I guess liberal homophobia can actually shift.

This was a school where I was assigned male friends in second grade because my teachers were worried that all my friends were girls. A school where I was called faggot on the playground every day, way before I knew what it meant. A school with many gay teachers, all of them closeted at school, some of them among the most hostile to queer students. A school where one teacher wrote a coming out letter to the student newspaper, and it was censored by the administration. A school that prided itself on its liberalism, its generosity, it's difference from the status quo. Structural homophobia, classism and racism were central to this pride. So here I am, wondering about my high school again, but through a more hopeful lens.

The break between possibility and collusion, and what does this mean for my sense of balance? Back at Pony, this guy watching the '70s porn says: They don't make cocks like that anymore.

Just look at those tan lines, he says—some people are born to be in porn, it's natural—we've lost those types of bodies.

I don't know how old he is, but I know he's younger than me.

I want to mourn the people we've lost, not the tan lines. The people we are still losing, inside or outside we are losing. A question of aesthetics is barely a question at all. When this is all we treasure, there is no way not to lose.

Someone wrote LOVE WINS on this receipt, and I kind of want to return it. Meanwhile, they're naming a new garden at the church down the street after a Macklemore song—yes, Same Love. Remember: when the Beatles said love is all you need, they were high. One problem with dissociation is that it's hard to pay attention to. Another problem with dissociation is when you're not.

How the critique of the market becomes the market. How art dies. How art is already dead. How art will never be alive. When the cops are friendlier than the gardeners, you know this world is really in trouble.

Back at Steamworks. I'm lying on top of this guy in his room, noticing the way my breath starts to match his, the in-and-out and the up-and-down, the side-to-side and the pressure towards and away, and when I open my eyes I notice I can watch our bodies in the mirror. That's hot, I'm thinking, it's really hot. Like I'm watching someone else but it's calmer. There's so much presence in this softness. I can't believe it's been years since I've done this. How is that even possible?

If the experience of loneliness inspires the search for connection, why is it that the search usually just results in more loneliness? Maybe desire is always a circle—sometimes you're inside, and sometimes you're out. But here's Carlos at my door—he's the guy from Steamworks. He actually called. Or, wait, he's not at my door, because he can't figure out where my building is, even though he's across the street. He keeps hanging up on me. The first time I thought his phone must have gotten disconnected, but then there's the second time.

I could go down and look for him, but maybe that's the wrong idea if he hung up on me twice, so I call Randy, and about 20 minutes into our conversation there's a call waiting click, and it's Carlos, so I buzz him up, but then he's not here so I call back, and I say are you in the building, and he says how could I be in the building? And I say oh, did you buzz the intercom, but he doesn't know how to do that. And then he does.

When he's finally here, I say what happened, and he says something about how the street numbers go in the wrong direction, and he couldn't figure it out, and I wonder if he's really high. I can smell alcohol on his breath, but he doesn't seem that drunk. He definitely moves like a junkie, swaying around my apartment, looking at everything really close and then far away, and then when we're sitting on the sofa he says: Are you vegan?

How did you know, I say, and he says: I was scanning all the words on the books. There's something sweet and childlike and strange but also affectionate about him, we sit there on the sofa kind of cuddling and he asks me lots of questions and I find out he ran away when he was 13, because his mother beat him so badly, he lived on the streets for most of the eighties, first in Bellevue and then in Seattle—now he's 49.

When I tell him I'm 43, he says really, and he sounds relieved. He says I thought you were in your twenties. I guess we're making out, and then we're in bed, and I'm sucking his dick for a while and then I move up to take a break and he says are you okay?

I'm just tired. And then we lie in bed again, looking up at the ceiling—he says do you keep the lights on when you go to sleep? And I'm trying to figure out how to tell him that I feel really comfortable, but I don't want to sleep with him. Because I'm worried I won't sleep. And if I don't sleep then everything's ruined.

So I get up to make tea, and then eventually he joins me in the kitchen, and then we sit together on the sofa again, now we're dressed. He says this is what I like the best. And I say me too. And it feels so sweet. Even if he does look disoriented again.

The next time he comes over, he brings me flowers—when was the last time someone brought me flowers? They're magenta with green centers, and he says: I spent a really long time trying to decide between these and the lavender ones because I'm such a dork. He uses that word a lot, like when I start telling stories about drugs, just so I can give him the opportunity to talk about drugs without worrying, and he says: I'm such a dork, I didn't even know that everyone around me was doing drugs when I was on the streets. I was a loner, he says, hiding out in doorways.

He tells me I look like one of the Monkees. Is that a good thing? And he smiles, and pets me. When I tell him I like to walk to Volunteer Park and lean against trees, he says we can fuck against a tree, and I think oh, this is going to work out. He likes to hold hands, and swing arms together. When we get to the park, I'm twirling in the field and he says are you sure you're 43?

Carlos is cold but he says he can take anything, and I wonder why he hasn't grown out of that mindset. He points out all the places that used to be woods in the '80s —this is where people used to sleep, he says. And this is where people used to fuck. But he's shivering, so I say let's go back to my apartment.

Back on the sofa, Carlos stands up all the sudden, throws on his jacket and backpack. I say are you leaving? At the door he says you know that thing when you really like someone? And I say you don't have to leave. And he says yeah, I do.

I could tell you that it ends here, even though it doesn't end here. We go to a movie, and Carlos can't believe I'm stretching. He's having a total breakdown about it. Even though I told him beforehand that I get up a lot or otherwise I end up in too much pain. He's already left ahead of me, and I've already thought: Okay, I guess this is over. After he looks at me with a combination of hatred and desire, and then walks out. He's not in the lobby, or outside the theater. But then when I get ready to turn the corner to go home, I see that he's on the opposite corner, so I go over.

Carlos doesn't understand why I don't have a boyfriend, and I don't understand how someone who's lived an unconventional life is still so bounded by conventional thinking. Maybe our best date is when we go to Goodwill together. He goes there every day after work because he collects vintage T-shirts. I love the way he watches me while I'm trying things on. He says you like sparkly things. You like purple. I find a beautiful sweater, and a hilarious wooden necklace, and a sequined blouse that I leave on my balcony for two months to get the smell of perfume out, in the sun and in the rain, until I realize it's hopeless, and I throw it away.

But before I put the blouse on the balcony, or maybe after the balcony, but before I throw it away, Carlos says he wants to take me out to a restaurant, and there aren't too many I can go to. But then we're at Café Flora, where I haven't been in years, sitting next to one another because Carlos says when he's on a date it has to be that way, and it is nice sitting next to him, rubbing his shoulder and kissing his neck, and the food is delicious. It doesn't feel like it's making me sick, at least not yet.

It's so noisy, Carlos keeps saying, and I think about saying we don't have to go out, we can do anything. We can do nothing. We don't have to follow some tired script about what it means to be dating.

Afterwards, we're walking back to my place and I say that was nice, and he says what—you enjoyed watching your date fall? I guess he means when he tripped for a second. I don't understand why he's holding onto that. I mean I understand it's because he's still in a traumatized place. From childhood. I wonder if that's why he got so lost on the way to my apartment that first time. Of course I understand trauma. It's something we can share. But I'm not sure he knows how to separate what's happening now from what happened then.

When we get back to my apartment, he says he's tired, so he's going to head home, when do I want to get together again? Sunday sounds good, I say. Sunday comes around, and I call him. And then I call him again. And then I call him again. And I guess that's the end.

Eventually I run into Carlos on the street. He's trying to arrange his backpack on a bike rack, and it's falling off. He definitely looks like a junkie. I go over to say hi, and he looks up at me. Hi, he says, and then he starts to move away like I might attack him.

This couple is playing a game where they unfold and refold the napkin into as many different shapes as possible, a metaphor for our times. Everyone's smiling at the toddler whose face is disappearing into the phone screen— migraines, depression, addiction, cluelessness, cultural amnesia, cancer, how cute.

How the present becomes a presence, a presence we don't want. How history works this way, our own histories, internalized without our consent. When we believe in the lie, we make it impossible to imagine the truth. This is obvious, but why is it not obvious?

The thing about the dance floor is we're all here together. But most people forget this. Or they're afraid. Fear creates its own kind of amnesia.

The thing about the dance floor is I'm fearless. To find this place in my body where I can let go of dreaming and just feel. Or let go of feeling and just dream. I lean against the wall and it's pounding, I'm pounding.

When the writing stops, and suddenly it feels like I have no access into how I actually feel. Or maybe I mean I can only feel. There's so much guilt in not writing. Or not writing what you want. Or not writing in the ways you want to.

People talk about the blood-brain barrier, but there's also the text-brain barrier, and the glory of writing is when you cross it. You're inside the gaps, and they are windows.

But then these are windows into other gaps, and you're stuck.

But the glory of writing is when you suddenly realize a way out, which is also a way in.

Sometimes I think the main tension among faggots is between those who see masculinity as a burden, and those who see it as a pleasure. Between those who see masculinity as a refuge, and those who see it as refuse. Masculinity as an ideal, and the ideal of refusing masculinity.

When I say a tension, I don't mean to suggest that there are two equivalent sides. The wrong side has already won. I'm trying to decide if this is desire I'm feeling, or just a sinus headache. I think it was desire, but then the headache took over. Trying to decide if this is a sinus headache I'm feeling, or just loneliness. Trying to decide if this is loneliness I'm feeling, or the end of hope.

Maybe that's what desire is for, to keep away this feeling. But what about when desire becomes this feeling? Maybe there's beauty in the way the words frame my face, but still my desire is only a shadow.

It's hard for me to imagine a gay culture that offers more than sex in the dark with strangers, when the one I've experienced usually offers far less. I don't want to give up on sexual splendor, but how can something be splendid when the boundaries always squash the potential? Say you're watching a movie, the way everything can be light and dark at the same time. The way a spotlight can feel like your heart. The way the brightest light can feel empty. The way the darkness can feel calm or terrifying. The way everything can happen at once, and nothing. The way your life can lead to a dead-end, and a dead-end can lead to something else.

I'm running down a street that becomes a bridge over the highway, to get to some mysterious and unwieldy fate.

This is a dream, right? Not exactly. I'm running down Lakeview to get to the mortgage broker before my mother has plastic surgery. Because she needs to co-sign the mortgage. This is a joke, right? Not exactly.

I've always lived in apartments that are crumbling. Beautiful apartments, but still they are crumbling. My last apartment was one of the nicest—a corner unit in a brick building from the '30s, with gorgeous hardwood floors, the original metal window frames that opened like doors, tons of light, a huge walk-in closet, and a sprawling living room. But the kitchen was tiny. There weren't any kitchen cabinets, and only a few built-in shelves, so I used one of those folding bookshelves that I bring with me from city to city, because they're always useful for something.

But that bookshelf got really crowded, so I would move one thing, and something else would fall. The kitchen faucet was always leaking, but the landlord would never fix it, because it wasn't leaking enough. I only had one tiny counter made of linoleum from the '60s or '70s that would peel away every time I cleaned it. Once my laundry lit on fire, and the landlord told me I shouldn't call the fire department—even though there was smoke pouring out of the machine, and my laundry had burned to cinders.

I could describe the whole horrible process that gets me into the middle-class dream I never aspired to, but I'd rather tell you about the feeling of waking up in this new place, waking up in this new place where I have a kitchen that I can hardly believe. I mean I can hardly believe it's so functional. Even just the galley counters that feel so spacious—before, I thought the granite was kind of tacky, but it's so easy to clean—and I love the way it sparkles in the light. All the cabinets, there are so many cabinets. I don't have to keep my blender on a chair anymore.

I spend my whole life in the kitchen, preparing all my food so I don't get sick. And still getting sicker. But it's nice to have a kitchen with room to dream.

I could tell you about waking up in this new place, and going into the laundry closet, my own laundry closet, with new machines that no one else has ever used. New machines that won't poison me. Full-size laundry machines that just barely fit, bright white against the pale green walls and purple marmoleum floors. Do you know about marmoleum? It's like linoleum, but instead of the usual chemicals it's supposedly made from just three plants, I can't remember which ones, on a jute backing instead of plastic.

I can close the pink door, and look up at the way the clear light bulb I put in the vintage light fixture creates a sparkling shadow in rings on the textured ceiling. So many shapes—it's almost like my own little kaleidoscope. Or, not a kaleidoscope, but the one that just has mirrors inside. I could tell you about being able to choose all the colors of my walls for the first time, bright pink and pale green and soft orange and creamy lavender and saturated yellow and only using no-VOC paint, and then waiting a month before moving in so everything had time to air out. It's not a big place—it's a one-bedroom that's maybe a little larger than my old place, and I didn't realize how much nicer it would be, until I moved in.

It's an ugly '60s buildings in a city filled with ugly '60s buildings, and when I first saw real estate signs from the window of my old apartment, which is diagonally across the street, I thought: Who would buy a place in that hell-hole? But then I went to an open house, for another corner unit, and it was one of the nicest places I'd seen that I could theoretically afford. I could tell the whole building had been gutted, but they'd kept the oversize windows, and they'd expanded the openness of the floor plans.

I never thought I would live in a '60s building, and I never thought I would want to buy a condo, but it seems like the best way to stay in this neighborhood that kind of works for me—on the same corner that I already know I love, even. I had the money for the down payment, because I inherited it from my grandmother. If my father hadn't died before her, I would have inherited nothing. This is how family works.

So the truth is that even before I move in, I go to a condo association meeting, and they announce that a repair project that was supposed to happen in 10 to 15 years needs to happen in a year. A repair project that was supposed to involve replacement of the windows, but now they're saying they need to tear out the walls.

They need to tear out the walls. That's what they're saying. Interior and exterior —all the walls where there are windows. Which is more than half of the apartment. This isn't a metaphor, why couldn't it just be a metaphor? A metaphor is so easy to fix.

Anyone who's ever dyed their hair black knows that black dye is impossible to get out, you bleach and bleach but it barely even gets lighter. So when I went to interview for a porn video, and the director told me I had to dye my hair for the shoot, I figured I'd use temporary black dye, since my hair was green and purple, and I needed to get it back that way as soon as possible. But the temporary dye just turned my hair gray, so I wore a bandanna to the shoot, which took place in a fake alley in back of a South of Market warehouse.

The director told me the safe word was BLUE, and that was about all, and then right after the camera started rolling the other actors pushed me to my knees and dragged me through gravel, and in the process the bandanna fell off. Then my costars saw my hair and said: Let's teach that punker a lesson. Now that I think about it, they were pretty good at improv, but at the time I was just scandalized that they decided to spray-paint the back of my favorite vintage red velour shirt without even asking me—I was supposed to act shocked about everything, but actually I was shocked.

Then they put me on a leash and said bark like a dog, so I did, woof woof, but when they got ready to push my face into a bowl of dog food, that was my breaking point. BLUE, I said—I'm vegan. Which would have been the best moment in the history of gay porn, so of course they edited it out.

One of my costars was some guy who said he was bisexual—apparently this meant he had to look at straight porn to get hard, and afterwards he kept talking about how his girlfriend was coming to pick him up, his girlfriend would be there soon, his girlfriend. Now I'd probably think he was tired but still incredibly hot, but when I was 19 my ideals matched my desires, so I just thought he was tired.

Around then I met Luke Sissyfag at a protest—he was wearing bright red lipstick and pearls, and I was in awe. He was risking being a stereotype, in order to become an archetype. We were both the same age, we were both in ACT UP, we were both obsessed with direct action activism and defiance, and I guess I was young enough that I thought this meant we should sleep together—I can't remember whether the lipstick smeared all over my face, but of course that's where it belonged.

Luke lived in Seattle, where there was actually a politic about being young, which kind of confused me because why would anyone want to be young? I mean anyone who was actually young. Luke came to stay with me in San Francisco, and it was like he already wanted to be boyfriends, and remember what I said about how my ideals still matched my desires—or maybe I mean my desires matched my ideals. Luke was so clingy already, and I really didn't know what was going on. I mean I knew what was going on, but I didn't like it. The next time I saw Luke was at the March on Washington in 1993, right after I met Zee at another ACT UP demo, and Zee said something about how he'd dated Luke, but it was over, so why was Luke following us around, and I didn't realize until years later that they'd just slept together.

Once, when I was driving cross-country, I drove through Lawton, Michigan, where Zee'd grown up, and then I went to the Zoo, the gay bar in Kalamazoo. It's hard to imagine anything that could make me as sad as a gay bar, except maybe a zoo. I don't go to zoos anymore, but I remember those signs as a kid at the National Zoo in DC that would show a dead sea lion cut open, and you would see all the pennies inside—don't throw pennies to the sea lions, this is what your hopes for good luck will do.

In high school, I went to the Zoo Bar across the street from the actual zoo, because they would serve teenagers pitchers of beer outside at the tables with vinyl red and white checkered tablecloths. For some reason the bar didn't card you outside, but inside they'd ask for ID, which doesn't really make sense because why did they want a bunch of 16-year-olds sitting outside and getting smashed? Except maybe then it would really be a zoo.

Sometimes I miss the sea lions in San Francisco—for years I refused to go to Pier 39 because I thought it was a scam—someone must have been feeding them to get them to stay there, right, it was just a covert zoo. But actually the sea lions took over the docks after the earthquake in 1989. They didn't even know it was a tourist trap. I love how they jump up on top of one another, but they can always sleep. I can't even sleep with someone else in my apartment.

The second time I did porn it was with Zee, when we were boyfriends, and I'd just remembered I was sexually abused, so I was taking a break from sex, but then Zee called me to do the video because his costar showed up too tweaked out—I did it because I needed the money, but then Zee got upset when I couldn't come, and I felt like a broken toy. Which is how I'd felt with my father.

Did I feel that way the first time I did porn too? I know I walked outside afterwards in a daze—I can still remember the glare of that dusty South of Market light. I looked out at all that light and I felt totally lost, like I was trying to land and why was it so hot out. Whenever someone says the weather in Seattle is the same as the weather in San Francisco, I know they don't know anything about San Francisco. In San Francisco, it's sunny every day for nine or ten months, and then you get two months of rain if you're lucky. In Seattle, if it's sunny for more than a few days in a row at any time except the summer it's like the biggest miracle of the century.

When I first moved to San Francisco, I would cross the street to get out of the sun—sometimes I even carried a parasol. In Seattle, I'll take off all my clothes on a 55-degree day just to try to get some vitamin D. I lived in San Francisco for 14 years, but I don't think I ever left the house in the morning unless I was up from the night before, walking through a deserted South of Market. No luxury glass towers yet, but it was already expensive in the early-'90s—or, it felt expensive. People in Seattle hear I wrote a book called *The End of San Francisco*, and they say you're right, it's over. But they don't know about that city that made me. It's the only home I've ever had. I moved back at the height of the last tech crisis, and still I was able to find as much vibrancy as I've ever experienced.

I remember going to visit a friend at 7 a.m. at the county jail after a protest—okay, so there's one time I got up in the morning, covering my eyelids in glitter to contrast the polyester plaid shirt and clashing plaid skirt, and then I was standing in line in a different South of Market, yes, here we are again, and I will say that the people in line were friendly, mostly women dressed up in their slutty best for their boyfriends or pimps, and I don't know why I'm telling you this to describe how I could breathe in San Francisco, except that I don't know if I'll ever be able to breathe like that again. The air in Seattle is better, but you need much more than air to breathe.

I didn't always do porn just for the money, the last time I did it because I thought maybe it would finally be hot. This guy in New York recruited me from my escort ad, he gave me some of his videos and said I could pick my costars, porn would be good for business—the guys in those videos were pretty hot, and I did need more business. But then somehow I ended up in a shoot with some ex-porn star who smelled like the end of the worst night of your life. And then after that I was in a scene with someone about my age, 20-something, who already looked like he was trying to look young.

When I first started turning tricks it was so I could make art and do activism and survive as far from mainstream consumerist norms as possible, that was all, it made the most sense, but by the time I got to New York maybe it had changed me—no, it was New York that changed me. Suddenly I was all alone—there were only a few other hookers who even admitted what they did for a living, but they said they were doing it as a career. I'd chosen to be a hooker so I didn't have to have a career.

In New York, the hookers at the top were the ones who thought they weren't hookers—I never wanted to be a kept boy because I didn't want to pretend I wasn't doing it for the money. Once I had this trick with the largest apartment I'd ever seen, an entire floor of a building in the West Village, and he spent most of the time telling me how he was trying to get rid of all the tenants upstairs, because there wasn't enough room for his art. He invited me to the Hamptons, and I said sure, and named a reasonable overnight rate, and he said oh, I could never afford that, I was just inviting you as a friend.

So I didn't go to the Hamptons. But then, later in the summer, New York had record-breaking heat, 106 or something, so I called him up and said let's go. When I got to his place there was another hooker there, and we got in the BMW with this trick who drove so fast it was like he was trying to kill you. When I say trick, I mean someone who's paying me, or in this case someone who I met when he was paying me, but I realize there's another meaning in the gay vernacular and it's always confused me.

Later this trick told me a story about how his boyfriend had died in a car accident, so maybe he was trying to kill us. Especially since he told the other hooker that his boyfriend had died in a pressure cooker accident. But actually the other hooker wasn't a hooker—he was Nan Goldin's assistant, not the one who developed the photos but the one who managed the studio, and I still have a photo he took of me in the Hamptons where I'm standing naked in the dark like a ghost with a towel by the pool that looks like it's floating.

Like Nan Goldin, right? She became one of my heroes after I saw that show at the Whitney, but then I went to a gallery show a few years later, and there were pictures of the gallery owner's kids. So that was the end of it for me.

Anyway, the trick took us to a party in the Hamptons like we were two exotic pets, here's the Dalmatian and here's the poodle. Like Matthew Bourne's *Swan Lake*, where the swans are all played by male dancers—another trick took me to that, the one who paid me monthly, and I smiled at the other kept boys but they were doing everything they could to pretend no one knew.

My last boyfriend said hands can be like pets, but you don't have to feed them, and I thought that was romantic. That was about a hundred years ago. My relationship model has always been friends that are like boyfriends, but we don't have sex, and then laughing after getting fucked against the wall by some stranger. But now I can't figure out how to have sex with people who actually care about me.

Towards the end of my time in San Francisco, I thought I might write a children's book about a vegan sea lion, one that doesn't believe in conventional gender roles—you know, that tired tale that all these sea lions on the docks are male, while the women fly south to have babies. There is a children's book for sale on Pier 39—it's about a sea lion named Chippy that's stranded on the highway a few hundred miles from the water, until it climbs up on top of a police car—see, the cops are always our heroes, even when we're sea lions.

In Seattle there's a program called Safe Place, where businesses put a rainbow police badge in their window to show that they'll call the cops if you're getting bashed. During this program, bashings of queers on Capitol Hill have only gotten more brutal, and it's no coincidence the program arrived while the Seattle Police Department is under federal oversight for violence against people of color. Let us save you, the cops say, so you can save us from oversight.

Bellevue Wives Matter, a silkscreen by John Criscitello tells us, and that's what the Safe Place program is really saying. Embrace us, and you can all become the wives of tech scions dreaming their suburban nightmares, as long as you leave behind Black lives. And now it costs

more to live on Capitol Hill than in Bellevue anyway—
the '90s are just a fashion trend. My rent was getting too
high to afford, and I escaped through upward mobility.

So now I pay my monthly housing ransom to a bank
instead of a landlord, and I can stay in the only neighborhood that might work for me. I won't pretend this hasn't
changed my life, and I won't pretend it's changed my life.

If you can't be so vulnerable in your writing that you
think you might die, what's the point of writing? I might
as well tell you about the guy in the park who stuck his
tongue in my ass when I wasn't looking, I mean I was on
my knees sucking someone else's dick so at first I didn't
know whose tongue this was—but then I realized it was
the guy with sores on his mouth who was in the dark on
his knees when I'd arrived, waiting for anyone. It always
scares me when people aren't concerned about anything
beyond their own desires, but it's not like this tells us anything new. All pets become animals, eventually. Maybe it's
the same thing with humans.

Then his tongue started to feel really good, except
that's when I realized it wasn't his tongue anymore it was
his dick so I pulled away, but afterwards I felt really gross.
This used to happen all the time, some guy's dick suddenly
in my ass, without my consent and without a condom.
How gay culture mimics the worst aspects of straight
masculinity, and will I ever escape I don't know.

A few weeks later some guy behind me on the street
was mumbling something about whether purple is a pastel,

and obviously it isn't, but I knew he was talking to me, and random people in Seattle never talk to me—and it really breaks my heart, it breaks my heart on a daily basis. People say it's the Seattle freeze like this is some kind of cute local popsicle flavor, but really it's just the gentrified gaze, the suburban imagination in the urban environment, the white picket fence in the eyes—people don't come to cities for that surprising interaction anymore, they just want to redraw the borders from the places they aren't even escaping.

When this guy, who turned out to be the one from the park with the clever tongue, at least when it was in my ass, but that's not what he spoke about it was the moment when we were on two sides of the same tragic guy, and how our hands met between that guy's legs—and why did I reach for those hands, really, why? I love public sex because of the possibility for a sudden connection, but now no one even wants that, so I grasp for anything. To me that night was just the most obvious indication that I need to figure out something else, but what, that's always the question, especially here, where most fags won't even talk to me.

This guy and I talked for an hour, on my morning walk through the park, and he was the classic example of someone who literally takes the same information as me, and develops the opposite ideas—and somehow he thinks this is what it means to connect. He went on and on about how you can't break the rules as an artist unless you know the rules. You need the training first, and then you can do something new, right? Prop up the same old system, in order to develop a new system. What a great idea.

I don't know why I didn't try to escape, I think it was the way that it all felt so strange that I thought it might be interesting. He told me he didn't read many books, but he read one that blew him away with its honesty, and of course it was Patti Smith's *Just Kids*. Has any recent work of art been more damaging to the urban imagination?

Patti Smith feeds us the same tired mythology about fame as a chain of coincidences, the one that says you can just go to the Chelsea Hotel with five cents in your pocket, and then suddenly you're a star. She feeds us that nostalgia for the glory days of a New York that never existed, the one where you fuck some guy who just stole a steak and it turns out to be Sam Shepard, and sure, that can happen, but fame is not a coincidence, it is a vicious mechanism and in order to succeed you must be complicit. Patti Smith wants us to swallow the myth of the successful artist as some kind of pure soul, which is one of the grossest lies ever told.

It turned out this guy from the park had been following me for months, I mean he didn't say it that way he just said he'd seen me around. But then I went to get my haircut, and he was the hairstylist in the next chair. He looked right at me, studied my clothes like usual so I smiled and said hi, Sam Shepard—no, he wasn't going to make me famous he just stole my steak I mean he stared right at me like I wasn't there. I said hi the next few times, but then eventually I gave up. I guess he felt like I'd rejected him, because he'd given me his number and I didn't call.

I'd already run into him again, before the salon, he was across the street and I yelled over. I said sorry for not calling—because even when I can't stand someone I feel a responsibility to be friendly. I told him I'd been feeling really exhausted, and he acted surprised by the never-ending chronic health problems that have defined my life for so long, because of course he was only listening to himself when we were talking, just like in the park on the night we didn't quite meet, the way no one quite meets in a cruising area but some not-quite-meetings are worse than others.

He said take care of yourself. So I did. By not calling him. Why was I trying to be nice to him anyway? Because everyone keeps letting me down. This is my romantic life, my romantic life right now. I want this story to have an ending, but also I want it to have a different ending.

When Kathy Acker drove up on her motorcycle and parked outside the South of Market warehouse where a friend of mine lived, I knew the image was what was driving her. She was a celebrity, so was this an act of kindness? Everyone was so excited. Maybe that's why I wasn't excited.

I was angry at the ways in which all these dykes were obsessed with Kathy Acker, and the ways she seemed to lead them on. My friend who lived in that warehouse was taking one of Acker's classes, where Acker said something about how sex between students and teachers shouldn't be taboo, and so my friend was convinced she was going to be the one.

But what was driving me? If I picture that warehouse, I see a barely disclosed need. Do you see how language hurts?

How the lack of language hurts more. How both of these things can be true at the same time. How language isn't everything. And how it is.

Inside longing, there is more longing. Why do I always end up here?

I can't decide whether I'm taking a shower to get ready to do something, or just getting ready to take a shower. Are we supposed to remember sex, or is sex about forgetting? And why is it that a memory of the best sex lasts a few days, but a memory of the worst sex can last a lifetime?

But then there's dancing. The way my body can spread out into the whole room. No, it's not my body, it's joy. This joy through music. This joy through the music in my body, my body in the room the room in my body and flying, that's what it feels like, if flying is my body giving way.

I'm rolling in the dust, spiraling up into a twirling stumble of joy, and someone says you make it all look so effortless. And this makes me feel effortless. And maybe that's the point—yes, to get to that place where my body doesn't need to hold anything closed.

We like to keep our nightmares separate from our dreams, but what if the nightmares are really closer to the waking reality? That feeling that something horrible is about to happen, and you can't do anything to stop it— that place before memory, which is really memory, but unremembered, that place where the only power you had was the power not to die. I mean I could have died, but I chose not to. I didn't want my father to kill me. This is just the truth.

The truth is also that he didn't want to kill me, and that's the harder part, because why make your child endure the horrors of war in the interior of upper-middle-class respectability, why take your child to the basement of despair, using the implements of torture I mean your body and the tools of the trade, in this case psychiatry and rape, psychiatry and rape and rage, psychiatry and rape and rage and control, control I would never have, control of my own body.

You think you cannot go on living, except you do. Did I imagine knives, or was he using knives? Did he drug me, and that's why I can't remember, my head shooting into the sky my body down there with his hands and all the pain I'm like two people, the head that is gone and the dead body cut open and everything goes white. Or do I remember the drug of dissociation. Of course he always had drugs around, he was a psychiatrist, that time when he told me you could inject drugs into the head, and no one would ever know, and I still don't know whether that's possible.

We can go back and forth between the living and the dead, the dead in our own bodies, our dead bodies, and we can't ever know anything else, anything else about this time when we're supposed to remember safety. An absolute. Absolute safety.

Of course absolute safety is never possible, but the feeling. We're supposed to remember the feeling. Trust as something that isn't just awaiting betrayal.

The problem of living. The problem of living in spite of it all. The problem of changing the larger world if we can't change ourselves. The problem of changing ourselves, if we can't change the larger world. The problem of existing in this world anyway. The problem of not existing.

This is too much, he says, just as I'm finally feeling something. Two minutes later I see him bent over a bed with his ass in the air, waiting for anyone to fuck him. Too much passion. Because we were making out—it finally felt like something that could make me feel, something that could make me feel something I want to feel. I mean I was feeling it. I was holding his head, tasting his mouth which felt so fresh, that tongue and the way my body can suddenly feel alive.

Too much pleasure, or too much pressure? Too much connection, or too much introspection? Too much expression, or too much transgression? I saw it in his eyes—he didn't just want to suck my dick, even if that's all he wanted to want.

I say you want more distance. I smile when he says yes. I always smile. I mean I always see it, but usually someone doesn't say it too, or not exactly. Just: I'm going to walk around. Or: I'll be right back. Or no words at all, just a sudden departure. If a body can be a confession.

We're not supposed to want what I want, not here, just more nothing where that nothing came from. This guy's nice enough, it's just that he's playing by the rules. What am I trying to create with my smile, a sense of play or a sense of place. Sex that isn't just a rotation of body parts. Instead I'm just trading one form of despair for another.

But then I wake up and I think about how everyone wants distance, and maybe that's the problem with all my relationships in Seattle—I want the distance to go away.

The one you love is one of the most dangerous myths, perfect for making our lives into sad ballads but I want something else. When did my relationships start to feel bounded by accepted limitations instead of grounded in the annihilation of expected norms? What happened to a shared place in and against the world, not just a few hours here and there?

A few hours of connection can always be erased. But what about the conversation that stretches on and on, that moves us into different shapes, shapes that hold our bodies better.

I don't believe in nostalgia because it camouflages violence. But there's one thing I miss about the early-'90, when I was first coming of age as an avowedly queer person in a world that wanted me dead, is that it felt like the people I met, I mean the ones I cherished, we all wanted closeness. We wanted distance from our parents and the world we hated, but we wanted closeness to one another. We were our own refuge. A refuge together not apart. A part of ourselves. And this failed us, sometimes even more than the worlds we'd fled, but I still believe in the same ideas—even if now I'm 25 years older I still want the same types of relationships, just without the perils of figuring ourselves out for the first time. I want relationships that always go deeper, or at least relationships where this is the goal.

It took me so long to learn how to initiate touch without worrying that I might cause irreparable harm to someone else. Sometimes I'm still afraid, but I've learned that I'll never find what I need if I don't at least try. If sex work helped me to learn how to assert boundaries, public sex spaces offered a realm where I could initiate touch without worrying about crossing an unseen boundary.

Now I need to figure out how to get the physical contact I need from people who actually mean something to me. How not to always be the one initiating. I don't just mean sex, I mean the casual touch that makes me feel like I'm alive. How to imagine a world where I always feel the way I feel when I start to make out.

Sometimes we create desire when it's not there, just to see if it could be there. Is this what it means to dream, or to stop dreaming? When distance and closeness feel like the same thing, and I can't tell if this is engagement, or disengagement. When someone says the body never lies, I wonder if they've ever had a body.

I'm pretty sure there's nothing as sexual for me as walking shirtless in the hot sun toward the pounding bass of a sound system telling me I'm about to dance. The vocal in the song says "Just like 1994," which it's not, not at all, but maybe when I get home I'll look up this song that proves nostalgia now zooms in right to the time of my formation—the nostalgia of the early-'90s was all about the '70s, but now we have both and neither one is true, as nostalgia can never be, but anyway I'm dancing, that's the important part. I'm dancing outside in the blazing sun, shoes and socks and shirt off, sweat dripping down my face underneath the sunglasses and hat that are protecting my eyes from too much light. I'm dancing down at the bottom of the hill, right by the sound system, but only about four other people are dancing with me.

It's strange how rave culture might be the only place where I pass unintentionally—what I'm passing as I'm not sure but I guess someone who might have come here on purpose. And eventually there's some shirtless guy who looks like a fag, dancing with a blow-up toy and a lot of the guys here look like fags until you watch them interact, but this guy's moves are too overtly campy and sexual to be straight and then he's dancing with me, I think, I think he's dancing with me—and, yes, maybe I've passed the point where I should be dancing this hard, but the good thing about the grass is I can just fall, over and over and it doesn't hurt, roll around but now I'm jumping in the air, twirling around until he's the one who's tired I hold out my arms for a hug we hug goodbye it feels so good all that sweat like a real hug I want to see him again.

There's nothing like an election to make you feel hopeless about the possibility for political change. I pick up a magazine promising America's Essential Recipes, and open it right up to PORK SCHNITZEL. I'm laughing so hard that everyone at the co-op turns around to see if they can be part of my laughter. And then I'm walking through a field of dandelions. Even if it's really just the grass between the sidewalk and street I will take this field while I can get it.

The news is always its own trauma, but when the news of the trauma echoes into our lives, past and present at once the open door never quite closes. Trauma as a curtain that billows around us, a wall we never quite break through. I mean trauma as a weapon. How to make oppression realize its redundancy. But oppression can never realize. Anything but oppression. How saying that something is structural means we need to take it apart or else it's a weapon we become.

How I can't go to a depoliticized vigil, I mean a vigil, which is always depoliticized, but walking past all the candles left out three days later makes me cry. How once we held political funerals instead of vigils. The power of grief in public spaces, but only if we're allowed grief on our own terms. How I can't listen to politicians telling me they're with me, and even worse is standing with people who are with these politicians. How assimilation even robs us of the tools we need in order to grieve.

Love is love isn't the most helpful rhetoric for those of us who grew up abused by the people who told us they loved us the most. They love us when we're dead, but they're not interested in taking care of us while we're alive.

I've never liked Robert Mapplethorpe's art, but I'm watching a documentary about him and suddenly I'm sobbing. Of course I knew the narrative ahead of time— but then: "You can tell how successful a show is by the sound in the room. On that night the room was silent."

The night of Mapplethorpe's last show. He couldn't attend because he was too ill. Everyone is peering into glass cases, and we're watching their watching. We don't know what they see—the recognition is ours.

How is it that recognition is always a shock? Recognition of self, recognition of feeling, recognition of impending death. Sometimes we think we don't need anything, and we need everything. And sometimes we know what we need, but we can't figure out how to need it.

This guy on the street says: How do you stay so blissed-out all the time? Which is one of the most confusing things anyone has ever asked me.

Confession: I just caught myself touching the leaves of a plant outside and thinking what is this made out of? One day, if everyone stops asking if I'm drunk, then maybe I'll drink again. When I was 16, I went out to a club for the first time, and I heard Nancy Sinatra's "These Boots Are Made for Walking" mixed with some industrial song, and for years I thought that was part of the industrial song.

Sometimes they put a deceptively attractive exterior on a fake building, and suddenly it looks real. When people move in, will they look like this too? On the playground, this kid says: I need a translator, I need a translator to eat tonight.

I'm kind of entranced by watching these guys in the park touch one another so gently. Then I notice one of them is wearing an NYPD T-shirt, and I want the world to end. Lying in the park trying to regain enough energy to walk home, I hear this guy circling around me, yelling in that language of conspiracy, internal made external, something about how if his people own this city how come he doesn't have shit and I know I should be thinking about the lack of mental health resources but instead I suddenly feel scared. Maybe because I drifted into something like sleep until the yelling woke me up. And I look at the other people in the park, one is staring at this guy and the other is still sunbathing—I'm getting ready to flee and I wonder if this is one of the reasons why we only have prison.

I'm watching a video where two guys are talking about sugar apples for Christmas. In bed. In German. One of them is wearing a wedding ring—he's caressing his lover I mean husband and the camera is caressing his ring. I should turn this off now.

Back to blurry streetlights, I do like blurry streetlights. Give me more blurry streetlights. New scene. One guy has feminist theory on his floor, but the camera goes for his ass. Everyone smokes everywhere—this is Berlin. I never realized I was sensitive to smoke until I lived in Berlin for a month, jetlag for two weeks and then bronchitis for the first time since I was a kid, and that was 16 years ago but now even if I walk too close to people smoking outside it gives me a headache.

Everyone speaks English perfectly here—you don't really need German to survive, says this guy who doesn't speak English perfectly. But why are gay men obsessed with white sheets? Everything they could never have, a lifetime supply of Clorox to bleach out all the come stains. Or maybe gay marriage keeps the sheets white.

I do like it when the guy with star tattoos on his arm says: Heterosexuality, what it that? Then he holds his cigarette to the other guy's ear as they start making out. I was straight in art school, he says, and they laugh. Okay, the making out is pretty cute.

But does this guy really have a huge cross tattooed on his back? Oh, they're laughing again—if only sex always included laughing, maybe we could live more for living. The guy with tattoos is telling the other guy he looks so much hotter in person, he should never bleach his hair blonde again. The other guy says he likes it blonde, it's going to be blonde again.

But what's going on now? The guy who used to be blonde notices scars all over the tattooed guy's arms—the tattooed guy is pointing out each of the places where he sliced himself—you do it this way, you do it that way. Cigarette burns—he's laughing.

It's so funny, isn't it, the other guy says. But it's like he's making fun of him, a challenge almost academic. Of course we underemphasize our wounds, those of us who must in order to survive. We laugh because this is what we know. I wish he would hold the guy with the scars, instead of challenging him to show emotion.

I keep rewinding this part that must be the key to why this movie matters, I mean suddenly matters for me. They're still talking about those scars. When was it, says the guy who used to be blonde, and the tattooed guy takes a gulp of his beer and says: Reality.

What he would have said if they were speaking in German doesn't matter as much as what we know now. Trauma in translation. Translation of trauma. The reality of living. Living with reality. How do we make this possible.

Sometimes I wonder if gated community is a redundant term. Creating boundaries around everyone who belongs, so that everyone who doesn't belong never will. I call Brian, and he surprises me by answering. Girl, where are you, she says, even though I'm calling from my landline. She's smashed. She says she's been thinking about me all day, she just wants to kiss my face—so then I'm getting ready to go to Pony, even though it's Pride.

I don't know if I've ever gone to a bar on Pride before. The best strategy is always to avoid as much as possible. But here it is. The moment I've been waiting for. Sure, Brian's smashed, but maybe this is an opening that will allow for a shift in our relationship. I need to take a shower first, even though Brian says come stinky. But stinky is not something I ever aspire to be.

Then I'm on the way there, and of course the whole street is blocked off in front of the Cuff, and the bass on the sound system is so loud that I kind of want to stay. Until the vocal comes on, and I realize they're playing "It's Raining Men."

The weird thing about being at Pony on the night of Pride is that everyone's so friendly. Usually people just stare at you and then look away, but now it's a constant stream of kisses and cruisy looks and Happy Pride, Happy Pride, so I figure I'll just smile and pretend that Pride can actually be happy.

Oh, there's Brian, in short-shorts and fuchsia lipstick, holding my hand and pulling me inside, where people are actually dancing, and then we're making out. We're making out on the dance floor. And then in the photo booth. And then back on the dance floor. It's what I've been waiting for, but I can't tell if it's hot—I'm so used to desexualizing my friends.

Maybe I'm not totally present. Until we're back on the dance floor, now I'm dancing and it's that flirtatiousness with movement that gets me high, then we're making out and I push Brian up against the wall right when "Tainted Love" comes on—yes, really, "Tainted Love"—and honey, we are singing it. And this is when it really gets hot, my tongue going up behind Brian's teeth and I can tell he loves that, he loves all this tainted love.

Every now and then Brian says something like: I love your lips. Or: You're one of my favorite people. And: Is this okay? I hope this is okay.

You're giggling, Brian says, and he's right, I am giggling. I'm giggling because I'm in my body. I'm giggling because I'm having fun. I'm giggling because can't it always be this way. I'm giggling because we're like a performance, and it's also like no one else is even here. I'm giggling because Brian's spilling his beer all over my leg.

Someone wants to piss with us in the bathroom, but that will make me pee-shy so I piss in the sink. Brian gets another beer—I don't know how he's going to drink another beer. We're making out again, and he's rubbing my chest, yes, do that, yes. I like that, and I can't tell if he backs away because it's getting more sexual, and whether I want it to be more sexual now or to wait until later. I mean I want to wait until later, but also I want to feel this, so I know it's there.

I like how you can just be here, Brian says, and I know he means the way I'm interacting with everyone like I've been partying all day too—I just go right there, it's in me, it's in my history and anyway these people are more on my level when they're smashed, I mean in terms of a readiness for intimacy, a lack of borders, an openness to possibility. Yes, there's still shade, but tonight there's less of a gap between yearning and softness.

Brian and I go on the patio where we can't believe it's still so light out, how is it still this light? I guess it's just the difference between inside and outside, but still somehow it's surprising. Brian has to piss again, and I think of going with him to make sure he actually comes back, but then I think that's weird so I wait for him outside.

Someone's fixing her makeup, so I ask if I can look in her mirror to see if my lips or cheeks are covered in Brian's lipstick, and her friend says what are you looking for, everything is perfect. Bleached blonde in a silver sequined dress like one of those women who's been in clubs for years I mean she's never left, I look in her eyes to see what drugs and we start dancing. The light is incredible, I say, and she says bring it down a little, I need something to cover this, and she points to her face, my eyes into her eyes and we're flying.

After a while it's clear that Brian isn't coming back, so I go to look for her, and there she is out front, all the way at the other end of the fence, making out with someone else. It's what I expected, but I didn't want to expect it so I decided to withhold expectation. It's not the fact that she's making out with someone else that bothers me, it's that she didn't come back to tell me about it first. I don't want to feel upset, but I feel upset. I don't want to walk back through all the smokers out there to get to her, and when I got to her what would I say?

I go back on the patio. Now I'm exhausted—what am I doing here? At least there's Amy, the woman in the silver dress. She says are you a Gemini—I knew you were a Gemini, I'm a Gemini, and there's that look in the eyes again, our eyes, and then there's John Criscitello, who comes over and says you look amazing, what's your secret?

My secret is that I'm completely exhausted all the time. My secret is that I'm so absurdly healthy, but why doesn't it make me feel better? My secret is that I don't have any secrets. My secret is that's not really true. My secret is that I still haven't figured out how to exist with or without gay culture. My secret is that I'm so desperately lonely most of the time. My secret is that I do love it when people tell me I look great. I mean I'm trying. I'm really trying.

But now none of this matters because the music is so good, and I'm back on the dance floor. Someone impossibly hot taps me on the chest, and says "You're breakfast," because that's the vocal—and she could be my breakfast, lunch, and dinner, but I don't want to do the same thing Brian is doing, I mean not until there's some communication between us, right, and now the communication is in my body throwing it down, flinging around, shrieking in that way that means there's nothing between my body and the world, this world of dancing and I know I should leave because now the smoke machine is on full blast, but I need to be here right now, with that dancing queen in the corner staring at me like damn, I mean she was doing that earlier too but then I went over to say hi and she couldn't speak.

Until I realize now, now's the time to go, while I'm feeling great again, before I crash, before it gets too late— I look for Brian again but I can't find him, so I figure I'll call when I get home. Amy's outside—she says I've been up for 48 hours, and you were just what I needed, I'm so glad we found each other. And then more kisses, more Happy Prides, and I'm out into the 10:30 p.m. but still not quite dark sky, where am I.

Back by the Cuff, there are so many discarded plastic cups in the middle of the street that it's almost like they were making a dance floor out of them. I'm thinking about how Pride is the one day of the year when fags can express their femininity, and still be sexualized. And how depressing that is. So maybe it's strange to say this is the only positive aspect of Pride I've ever experienced.

And then there's that feeling that people are closer to the possibility of experiencing connection when they're smashed, and therefore further from the possibility of experiencing connection. This is what it means to celebrate. How desire and disgust can feel so closely related, surrounding self-actualization with self-hatred. Is this just true for queers, or for everyone? How a universal experience is universally impossible.

But I had fun, I'll admit it, I did—I'm thinking I need to look up that "You're breakfast" song. I'm thinking that I don't want to call Brian and act like I wasn't annoyed, but how will I do that? I'm so used to acting like I'm not annoyed, and how this shuts me down.

I get home, and I call Brian. Voicemail. I love voicemail. I can always say exactly what I want.

Happy Fourth, he says with a grin as the explosions are going off behind us—or behind him, and in front of me, if I have to think of it that way, and I don't. The explosions are going off, and even though I know that everything about this day is wrong I also know this feels romantic, I guess, leaning into him as he reaches his hand into my pants, and you know how usually I don't like it when someone touches my dick if I'm not hard, but I'm so turned on by him anyway that it doesn't matter, nothing matters except that this is happening, here in the park where I wasn't expecting it because of all the people around. And maybe that makes it hotter—no, what makes it hotter is that it's him, whoever he is, something about his grin that's for me, the way he's sitting there when I arrive and there's no hesitation.

You know how I am when there's just a hint of an indie aesthetic in a place where it rarely exists, I mean he's someone I would want to have sex with somewhere else, anywhere—although we're here and when he dives for my dick I still wonder if he's straight in the way I always wonder if someone's straight when he's really into me. When I'm really into him. And then when he lifts his hands, maybe he's trying to free his head from my grip but how can I help holding him there—eventually he stands up and then it's my turn to dive, he's moaning right away and that's the way I like it.

Dude, you've got me so close already, he says, the problem of masculinity and language, masculinity in language, but also I can't claim that I'm not complicit, the way my tone becomes everything I learned from being a hooker for over a decade, masculinity the only thing that makes money, the skills I learned there that served me well in gay male sexual spaces too, but then there's something else that comes from inside, the way masculinity can be a language too if we get rid of the language it owns. If we get rid of everything but my lips around his dick a craving. Just the way I stand up, and we're finally making out. Just the way I'm holding his head and maybe masculinity can be pure.

First he reaches around for my ass so I stand up and say do you want to fuck me, I mean I know he wants to fuck me because that's what that means, those eyes the way he's looking at me but I'm trying to tell you that I'm wearing a purple velvet hat and all my earrings, a magenta jacket with matching French cuffs peeking underneath, and purple velvet pants, and this is what he likes, I think, or at least he likes me, but still there's a part of me that always thinks the only way I can become desire met is if I channel the drive of sex into some form of masculine demeanor that matches what I think they want and where am I, in this demeanor, and where am I lost?

I say let me get a condom, the way I always make sure I'm prepared, because sometimes when I don't think it's going to happen it happens, the fireworks louder now, people just 20 feet away, I say do you want to go somewhere but he doesn't, he wants to fuck me here, right behind this statue, I can tell that's part of the attraction, that grin and those eyes, he says are you negative.

Yes.

Are you on PrEP.

No.

I am.

Let's use a condom just in case, I say, when really I mean in any case, how the casual must be maintained in order for language not to get in the way, go slow at first I say, even though there's no pain it's just his dick inside and then I'm already grinding, his hands right at my hips he says you want me to give you my nut, and before you remark on how the cheesiness of porn has conquered imagination, I'll tell you that I love the feeling of his hands on my hips, holding me against him as he comes but really I want his hands all over me, arching back my hat starts to fall, he catches it, says don't lose the hat, no that's after I come so hard I'm gasping, I mean first there's the arching back up against him, then the moaning, then the realization that I'm really loud, then the laughter of sex when it's really connected, how I can't help it, how don't lose the hat feels like intimacy, but especially afterwards, when he says: We're badass. The explosions going off, now they're louder but so are we.

And he's right, actually, I mean usually I don't think of it that way, and certainly not in that language that still makes me think he must be straight, even though he's on PrEP and straight guys don't take PrEP, how I'm still confused about someone's desire for me, how to recognize it, but when he says we're badass, yes there's the we that's acknowledged but also the way I think about these spaces now—the habit I can't shake, the desperation mixed with loneliness and despair, the longing for something else, the search for other options, the hopelessness of ever finding what I need. But the way my desire always leads me here, and sometimes the joy that's irreplaceable.

If we lived in a different world, this would just be what people do. And, if we lived in a different world, we would have more options. And we would have more options for this. But when he says we're badass, he's talking about the world as it is now, the way he's just leaning against a statue so close to the public eye, the way people are celebrating our nation's bloodthirsty birthday, the way the relative darkness is a shelter but at any moment we could be exposed. And we don't care. Or maybe we do care, but also we need this, we need one another—and, yes, he's right, this is a kind of bravery.

The way I cross the street in San Francisco, which is really the highway to get to the Delaware beach condo where I went as a kid, and then I'm in a strip mall near where I grew up in the DC suburbs, and I'm going to an afterhours club in New York. But do I mean everything is in present tense, or everything is present? The way every place is another place, which is another place too, and in the dream you move from one to another even when you're still. I look at the plants on the shelves by the window that I thought had died a long time ago, and the leaves are cascading toward me in the light, and I'm trying to remember whether I've ever seen plants this beautiful, and when I wake up I realize I was in my childhood bedroom.

I suppose it was inevitable that I would have a dream where Donald Trump hires me as a hooker. At first I think I'm supposed to go to the Four Seasons, but then I realize wait, why would Trump pay for a hotel room? Obviously it's the Trump Plaza. I get there, but then I can't remember the room number. Luckily a friend of mine is in charge of the front desk—she says Trump is always in room 3 or 4. Both are on the first floor just past the lobby, and the door to 4 is open, so I go inside. I'm kind of wondering why Trump isn't worried about getting discovered, I mean isn't he running for President? But then I see that one empty room leads to another empty room, and he's in the third room on the bed, naked and drunk, wrapped in sheets. He says hi, honey, kisses my shoulder, and I think oh, I guess this isn't going to be that bad.

When you say I love you to someone you've loved, but you don't know if you love them anymore, this is its own form of sadness. Or you don't know if you love them in the same way, which is the same thing as not knowing if you love them anymore, or almost the same thing. Is this love or is this loss, and what is the difference? The unvoiced question, and what is the cost of keeping it unvoiced. How this is its own form of sadness too.

It's too hard not to give up, and it's too hard to give up. I want to believe that relationships can hold me, but instead I just keep holding onto relationships that never really become relationships. Is it better to hold onto what will never become what you want, maybe if what you want may never become. Wanting is so much harder than not wanting, and yet not-wanting is a trap door so either way you will always keep falling.

If I give up, I will never feel my body without loss, and yet if I don't give up will I always end up feeling lost? I don't believe in answers, and I don't believe in never finding answers. I know that I don't want too much, and yet I don't know that everyone I want doesn't want too little. When you give up, but still you hold on, just in case, what is the cost of this holding on?

So I see one of my closest friends for four days, four days after not seeing him in over a decade—four days like a vacation, still the same problems in my life but someone to talk to. What this allows the body to imagine.

And then as soon as Andy leaves I feel lost. Why is it so hard to find the relationships I need in everyday experience? How we carry loss until it becomes another loss.

This burden of unburdening—how to speak until the body un-collapses. How to speak until there isn't only a wound.

When someone says they feel all the same things you do, all the joy and camaraderie, the playfulness and intimacy, the connection and depth of awareness, but still, it's really just too hard to make plans ahead of time, it makes it feel like an obligation. Instead of just fun.

But then if we don't make plans ahead of time, we never see one another. What is just fun, I will never understand this.

Alyssa and I used to get together once a week—it was a commitment, a commitment that helped me to feel like this might build into the type of relationship I need, I mean it was building, I thought we were building, I thought we were building something. But then once a week felt like too much for her and now I'm left with nothing.

Shouldn't a friendship include obligation? If it's really a friendship. If it's going to develop. Or, if it's going to remain. Shouldn't a friendship remain?

And then there's Brian. We went to the park a week after Pride, when Brian was getting over a cold—we both said we wanted to make out again, once he was feeling better—he said he would have a lot more time to hang out over the summer, not as many obligations, we could get together a lot. And then I didn't hear from him for two months. And, after two months I only heard from him because I called to say what's going on? But still no plan. Just the oh, I've been so busy. With camping trips. Applying for jobs.

But we live four blocks away from one another. Brian has a dog. He needs to walk the dog. I've already told him he can just ring me from downstairs when he's walking by, just to say hi for a few moments, I mean just as one way to stay in contact on a regular basis. Anything but nothing. Why does everything lead to nothing?

I haven't written about Adrian recently, so maybe it's ironic that I'm writing about him now because when we're having dinner or maybe lunch, I think it's lunch, something between afternoon and evening, and he says he hates it when people get in relationships just so they have something to make art about, and he's talking about Graham, and their breakup, and how he told him not to make art about their relationship.

Adrian says he wouldn't write about an ex, because they would still be friends, and he wouldn't want to lose that friendship. I've lost relationships because of my writing, but the truth is those relationships were already over. When people become more concerned with how they're being portrayed than about working on our relationship, then I know we don't really have a relationship.

You don't want to hurt someone you care about, but what if writing in the deepest and most honest way possible is what keeps you alive? There is a difference between personal vulnerability and public disclosure, but I don't know if I want one without the other.

As the relationships I crave become more and more difficult to find, as the consistency I need from other people just seems basically impossible, the one thing with which I have a consistent relationship is my writing. So it's hard to take any part of that away.

Of course all this leads to Adrian—you know, you're probably in my next book, I say—I mean especially if it starts with my emotional opening at Pony, and you were there, right, you were there the next time I walked into that bar. And you said: What are you doing here? And I said I'm trying to have an embodied self in a world of fags, it's an exploration—I'm trying to figure out a way to feel connected, even with all the limitations I know so well.

Adrian knew those limitations, but also he was there anyway. He found me because of my writing. That's what enabled us to become friends on a deeper level, right away. My emotional vulnerability. His knowledge of my history. His engagement with all of this.

So now I do have fags in my life, I've succeeded at that. But the other part of this exploration—how to have sex with people I actually talk to, or people who actually talk to me, how to have a sex life that matters, that matters to me and to my sense of embodiment and safety, emotional and physical connection, my place in the world as a creature of sense and sensuality—sometimes I feel like giving up. I feel like there's no possibility.

But there's a possibility right now, because I'm writing. This is what writing means to me. Sometimes I write something, and then I have to think about it more. And sometimes I think about something, and then I have to write about it more. There is so much potential joy in the dynamic between writing and thinking, thinking and dreaming, dreaming and fear, fear and loss, loss and writing. I thought of changing joy to something else, but I think I do mean joy. Isn't this the point of writing—the gasp of recognition, the recognition of the gasp?

So maybe it makes sense that I'm feeling this emotional opening now, when I'm thinking about this conversation, this emotional opening that allows me to write, to write about someone I love who told me he hates it when people do that. He told me he was talking about music and visual art, and not writing, but also he said: I would never do that, I would never write about someone like that.

But then he said he wasn't worried about what I would write.

I spend the whole day with Adrian. We start in my apartment—Adrian helps me to put away my groceries, and I heat up some food for him. Then we walk to the park, and the sun actually comes out. Then we go to a café to get Adrian some tea because he's quitting coffee. And then we go to Dean's house so I can take a bath, because my bathtub has a hole in it. So I'm getting it replaced. Which means tearing out the walls. But at least it's just the shower walls.

After my bath, Adrian and I walk to a restaurant to eat more, and then we come back to my apartment, and Adrian flips my mattress for me. I'm saying there's comfort in the mundane, in the domestic, but also the shift in locations, the way you communicate in different ways in different places. In different moods. In different spaces. The way sometimes I'm talking nonstop, but why am I talking nonstop, oh, I think I'm excited to be with Adrian. And sometimes Adrian's talking nonstop, and I know he's excited to be with me. And sometimes both of us can barely speak, but even then or maybe especially then there's this comfort—not always, but always there's the awareness, maybe it's there even when it's not there. And that's what a relationship can mean. How can I not write about that?

It's amazing how these queens in *An Evening at the Garden of Allah* tell their stories, and they feel so much like mine. These are queens of my grandmother's generation, but they sound like people my own age who I met in the 1990s. The camp banter to disguise pain. To surprise pain? To survive pain. The hooker world view. The same narratives of surviving abuse, and empowering ourselves through the pageantry and camaraderie of outsider cultures—but this is 1930s Seattle they're talking about.

Yes, there's a dated clueless racism, but I'm not sure there's any less of that in Seattle now. An overinvestment in middle-class norms. Denigration of femininity among the feminine—all that certainly sounds familiar.

To be honest, it sounds like queens in the 1930s supported one another a lot more than queens do today. Vilma says, "A queen was anyone who was gay and didn't try to hide it," and I'm still with her.

Thinking about how the demand for closure in writing often just means the death of insight. In life, though, closure means more insight, right? At least this is what it feels like when I imagine it.

What would happen if there was an earthquake, asks the ice cube. We would need a really good insurance policy, says the ice cube tray.

What about a fire, says the ice cube. You know the answer to that, says the ice cube tray. I just want to be prepared, says the ice cube.

I can protect you in a flood, says the ice cube tray. At least for a while.

What about a hurricane, asks the ice cube.

I don't know about a hurricane, says the ice cube tray. They're getting worse and worse.

I still don't understand how anyone could use an icemaker, says the ice cube.

It's definitely not something I would try, says the ice cube tray.

It sounds so painful, says the ice cube.

I feel you, says the ice cube tray. But do you know what they do in a restaurant at the end of the night?

What, says the ice cube.

They throw all the ice out onto the street, says the ice cube tray.

I don't believe you, says the ice cube.

And do you know what happens in a bar, says the ice cube tray.

You know I don't like to think about drinking, says the ice cube.

They pour all the ice into the urinal, says the ice cube tray.

Now you're just trying to upset me, says the ice cube.

So the library took away the benches outside. The benches that were bolted into the metal walkway. I used to love how people would be there at all times of the night playing music or checking their email or doing drugs. I would watch from the window of my old apartment, and it actually felt like a public space. I even imagined that the library meant it that way. It made me love Seattle.

Now people nod off on the stairs, or in the small patch of dirt between the library and the sidewalk. Sometimes people piss or shit or shoot drugs in the carport of my new building, or try to sleep there to get out of the rain—I'm at a condo association meeting, and someone says that if we don't get a fence around the parking lot then he'll just shoot homeless people when they try to use the carport as shelter. He says it as a joke, but how is this a joke.

Seattle is the fastest-growing city in the country, and everyone just wants fences. I look up at the balcony of the Starbucks popular for gay men, and see five cops with shaved heads staring down at me. Every bad porn movie starts with whatever it is in their eyes, exchangeable bodies or exchangeable lives. There's too much overlap between cops and gay men, I mean this in every way possible.

One problem with Seattle is the tourists aren't any worse than the people who live here. I find a pink polka-dotted flip-flop in the street. When I get closer, I realize the polka dots are actually hearts. The thing about desire is that sometimes when it falls away this feels like a relief. And sometimes it feels like a gap in consciousness.

I put the red bulb in the bathroom heat lamp fixture, and now I kind of just want to stay in the bathroom. There's a person that's addicted to a bridge, this kid is telling someone—a bridge, he's addicted to a bridge. What is the difference between desire and craving? What is the difference between craving and longing? What is the difference between longing and hope?

We lament the loss of bohemia, and its replacement with some kind of nostalgia for nostalgia, a disengagement in the midst of engagement, but it's also possible that's what bohemia has always been. A kind of posturing that can lead to a dream of connection or a walled-off insufficiency. How do we imagine what we can no longer imagine?

When I was a kid, adults would lean down to say: You're so idealistic. Like this was only something a child could be—you'll grow out of it, they told me. The problem is that most people do.

Who invented the refrigerator, asks the ice cube. Someone who doesn't like us, says the ice cube tray.

What about the microwave, asks the ice cube. Someone who doesn't like anyone, says the ice cube tray.

Sometimes I feel like you're speaking French to me, says the ice cube. That's because you're a romantic, says the ice cube tray.

Have you ever seen *The Ice Storm*, asks the ice cube. I don't think it means what you think it means, says the ice cube tray.

I'm alone in the park, looking up at the stars yes the stars are beautiful tonight we don't usually see the stars at this time of year and something comes running up maybe I scream?

Oh, it's a lost dog. Maybe it's too easy to feel like we're all lost dogs tonight, but then I'm lying in the cold grass staring up at the stars to ground me and tears I didn't expect tears I mean I believe in none of this but still tears. I'm saying I didn't expect to be shocked on election day— I was prepared for the violence of liberal optimism, but not for the violence that everyone can recognize.

The next night I hear the protest from my apartment. I didn't expect to want to go, but then somehow I find myself rushing to find it, walking fast almost running for blocks and blocks past all the people walking uphill away from the protest, but where is it going? Toward the highway or the University Bridge so I run walk almost 2 miles to catch up and there are others run walking with me— we keep getting to the cops so we think we're there, but we aren't there yet. There aren't usually people walking up or down this part of 10th it's mostly just cars but tonight there's a festive feeling I'm kind of excited I mean even if I don't make it I already feel better.

But then I do make it, just as the protest gets onto the University Bridge, takes half the bridge and then the whole thing, still several hundred people and when I arrive I'm already covered in sweat under my winter hat coat sweater shirt tank top but it doesn't feel draining it feels great. I hope we're going toward a highway ramp but then we head into the University District and I guess all these people have been marching for hours already, all the way from downtown that's miles but everyone still seems excited.

The chants are predictable but not bad, mostly Not My President and Hey Hey Ho Ho and My Body My Choice and then later Pussy Grabs Back and Black Lives Matter—it's anarchists and students and anarchist students but mostly probably non-anarchist students, mostly white people, yelling Out of the Dorms and Into the Streets, and when we walk up University and turn, get stuck in the dark on campus where it's Out of the Halls and Into the Streets. And a young transmasculine person asks if they can march with me after I introduce myself, we bonded a while back and now we're pals in the way that in a very straight space those of us who are visibly queer can find comfort in one another.

And the march goes down frat row, where it becomes Out of the Houses and Into the Streets—see, the crowd knows the vocabulary of university housing and I'm skeptical of these chants I mean why are we asking the gawkers packed on gender-segregated balconies of conformist hyper-patriotism to join in?

Except then I realize this is probably the only time the people in this crowd can take charge on frat row. So why not take charge? And then my new friend says they joined the march after hearing Out of the Sidewalks and Into the Streets—so, okay, I guess sometimes those chants work.

But who knows where we're going—I mean we're marching in circles but there's energy. When we turn onto 50th I look back and the march is several blocks long, the whole street across and this is a wide street a thoroughfare it looks like the march has doubled in size and I try to count but can't—I'm guessing at least 1000 and we're headed back to the highway for several standoffs with the cops, a few sit-ins in the street, a few times almost taking a ramp and then it's time for me to head back.

I need a bathroom and look, there's one in that park, actually open. And then one of the only restaurants in town that probably won't make me too sick, for cucumber juice and quinoa minestrone where I'm so hot that even after removing all my layers I want to take off my shirt although I guess you can't do that in a restaurant, not even after bonding with the staff about the exhilaration of the surprise protest and here's where I'll tell you that I don't usually go to protests like this anymore—I barely even go to protests because the ones that would mean something to me are too dangerous for the fragile ecosystem that's my body I mean I'm already a wreck all the time so why risk destroying myself in pain on so many levels when I probably won't even be inspired or feel useful anyway.

Who knows what will happen in a few days, but tonight I don't feel destroyed, I feel energized. I feel like I'm a part of something. Even though if I sat down with these people, mostly straight white late-teens and 20-somethings chanting Not My President like they don't even realize that no president will ever be ours—I mean they might even have been celebrating if the other vicious imperialist candidate had won and what would that have felt like. Luckily I figure out an intervention, thanks to a post on Twitter from Black Autonomist just before I left the house—so when the crowd chants Not My President, I reply with NO MORE PRESIDENTS, back and forth as if it's call-and-response. I catch a few of the straight anarcho boys smiling at me I mean I know how to use my voice I'll admit I think of romance but that's as far as we will go. I'm saying that if I sat down with these people—no, we were not sitting down, except in the street, we were a chain of bodies in motion emotion and I don't want to overstate the possibilities but there are possibilities.

Do you believe in justice, asks the ice cube. Of course not, says the ice cube tray. Otherwise we wouldn't be stuck here.

He says you're wild, and I am wild. The magic of some-one else's desire reflecting mine. Other people's words can make your words possible. I mean other people's words can make your worlds possible.

This is when I notice people are standing back and watching us like a show—I think it's because of the abandon but also the back-and-forth, the mutuality. The panting and the freedom, the playfulness and the hysteria, the adventure of opening into each other's arms, the way I squeeze him so tight and I can feel his breath shifting mine. When I wrap my arms around him, and I feel so strong.

The way desire can create safety—that's what this feels like, even I mean especially when I'm getting fucked against that tree right by the pathway yes I'm almost in the light and anyone could walk by, but this is what safety feels like. It's an illusion, but when you get there in your body there's nothing else.

The transition between a houseplant, and a tree growing in the middle of your living room. The transition between the music you play in the morning, and the music that makes you feel like you're mourning. Can I just be honest for a second, and tell you how much I hate technology? There, I feel better. I'm walking down the street, and some guy stops his car, rolls down the window, and says: That's a bright coat, do you know where I can get ecstasy?

I guess I could tell you that I bought a cellphone, I bought a cellphone just to try the hookup apps. I resisted it for so long, but what are the other options? I could tell you that the first person I hook up with says Mattilda, that's a beautiful name. So that's a good start. And the second one invites someone else over to fuck my face—the more, the better. And the third one fucks me in an alley, which I could probably do every day. I mean if it was with him. But now I know he's never going to write me back again. There are a few others, but now it feels like it's done. I mean I say nice things to people, but no one replies. How do people do this all the time?

When I can use the possibility of connection in this particular way to keep me connected to the possibility of connection in the world, even if nothing happens then this makes me more present. The way I can look at this thing and feel a sudden rush, and then look out and see the world around me in that way too. Not that obsessive craving for escape but a curiosity about the possibilities. Except when there aren't any possibilities. So when I try to connect, and no one responds, which is most of the time, it doesn't really feel like another option. Another way of trying to connect, to add to the list with Steamworks and the park and craigslist, and maybe four unsatisfying ways are better than three, I don't know.

Listening is a form of embodiment. When you're listening deeply, not just to what you're hearing, but to what's inside. What's around the insides. If I can sense into what Adrian needs then I can also sense into what I need. Maybe I'm saying that friendship is a form of embodiment. A way into breath. How I can feel more when I'm with you. The way I'm standing here in the park, sensing into everything at once. A current moving through my body—it's always there, right? How to get to the place where I can always feel it.

This guy is having a meltdown on drugs—from the distance it looks like a cross between dancing, masturbation, and prayer. He's shirtless, flinging his arms while touching himself—there's a cyclical rhythm, but also he's scratching for what's not there.

If I say possession, then you know I'm thinking of my desire, and a bad movie. He might collapse at any moment, but for now he's still flinging, and I'm watching from my apartment. I want him to win, but he's already lost.

What gives you hope is one of the most annoying questions. It's as if you have to feel hopeful in order to live.

It's been decades since I transformed I hate myself into I hate the world. I can tell the difference between the news, and a noose. I can figure out if something in the oven is burning, or if the oven's burning. I can taste the difference between a beet I bought at the store, and one I harvested from my own garden. But this doesn't mean I have a home.

There's the sigh, and the headache, the internal facing eternal external, the infernal. When something's too depressing to write about, that means you need to write about it. How the cities where we've come to survive now foreclose the possibilities for connection in the spaces and places where we've always found it.

If I say there's nothing soft about escape, I mean the open heart of broken-heartedness. If there's always the possibility for more longing, what does this say about possibility?

First I believed that desire was evil, and then I believed it was a map. But no one believes in maps anymore.

Acknowledgements

As always, I want to thank the brilliant and generous writers and friends, friends and writers who gave me detailed feedback on the manuscript: Jennifer Natalya Fink, Corinne Manning, Jory Mickelson, and Katia Noyes, a million thanks to you! And, to Amanda Annis, who helped me clarify my goals and sharpen the prose. And, to Anastacia Reneé, Adrian Lambert, Andy Slaght, and T Clutch Fleischmann for reading the manuscript at a later date, and so thoughtfully adding their important insights in key areas.

Every book I write comes about in surprising ways, and this one in particular benefited from three invitations. In 2014, Margaret Tedesco invited me to contribute an essay on the occasion of an exhibition by Jaimie Healy and Sahar Khoury at 2nd Floor Projects in San Francisco, which eventually became the beginning of *The Freezer Door*, but I didn't know this yet. Generally with a new book I just write and write, without imposing any structure, until I eventually have a sense of what it is, and, when Corinne Manning and Anca Szilagyi invited me to feature at the Furnace Reading Series, which consisted of one author reading a story about Seattle to completion each month, I decided to take a look at the sprawling manuscript I'd been working on, to extract something of promise for the February 2016 reading, and that really became the beginning of *The Freezer Door*. When Corinne broke the text down to shape it into a chapbook for the event, well then I realized it should stay broken down. And, when Peter Mountford invited me to read at the Hugo Literary Series in November 2016, and Hugo House commissioned me to write a new piece on the theme of "Animals," after I wrote that piece, which ends with, "I want this story to have an ending, but also I want it to have a different ending," I knew I had an arc for this book.

For tangibles and intangibles: Kevin Darling, Andy Slaght, Joey Carducci, Adrian Lambert, Tony Radovich, Jed Walsh, Sarah Schulman, Jesse Mann, Jessica Lawless, Dana Garza, Yasmin Nair, Meghan Storms, Alyssa Harad, Nick Arvin, Alexander Chee, Lauren Goldstein, Jessa Crispin, Sara Jaffe, Marisa Hackett, Carley Moore, Conner Habib, Masha Tupitsyn, Lara Mimosa Montes, Cari Luna, Matthew Schnirmann, Jacob Olson, Zoë Ruiz, Eric Stanley, Ananda La Vita, John Criscitello, Karin Goldstein, Kristen Millares Young, Chavisa Woods, Steve Zeeland, Jason Sellards, Tree Swenson, Rob Arnold, everyone at Hugo House, Karen Maeda Allman, everyone at Elliott Bay Book Company, Book Workers Union, Rebecca Brown, Elissa Washuta, Dean Spade, Calvin Spade, Griff Tester, Marcus Wilson, Felicia Luna Lemus, Jessica Hoffmann, Daria Yudacufski, Alex West, Jessica Mooney, Zee Boudreaux, Tommi Avicolli Mecca, Justin Vivian Bond, Sophia Shalmiyev, Jess Row, Keidy Merida, Sarah Neilson, Devyn Mañibo, Michelle Hart, Cara Hoffman, Madeline ffitch, Daniel Allen Cox, David Naimon, Brian McGuigan, Lisa Factora-Borchers,

Rigoberto González, the Poetry Project, Hatlo and everyone at the So Queer residency at Town Hall, On the Boards, the Estate of David Wojnarowicz and P.P.O.W., Tara-Michelle Ziniuk, Maggie Nelson, Andrea Lawlor, Wayne Koestenbaum, and anyone else I may have inadvertently forgotten—in spite of the length of this list, I'm sure there are many.

For publishing excerpts of this book, in various forms and at various times: *Boston Review*, *Fence*, *Evergreen Review*, *Berfrois*, *Meetinghouse*, *A Gathering of the Tribes*, *Make/shift*, *Ploughshares*, *Animal Shelter*, and Twitter, which helped me to think about text out of context.

To Hedi El Kholti for taking on this project, and designing such a stunning book from start to finish. And, to everyone at Semiotext(e), including Chris Kraus and Janique Vigier—I'm so honored to be part of the Semiotext(e) legacy of destroying literature by creating our own literature.

No writer is a writer without other writers, and so I'm thankful for all of you, really. Let's do this together.

ABOUT THE AUTHOR

Mattilda Bernstein Sycamore is the author of three novels and a memoir, and the editor of five nonfiction anthologies. Her memoir, *The End of San Francisco*, won a Lambda Literary Award, and her anthology, *Why Are Faggots So Afraid of Faggots?: Flaming Challenges to Masculinity, Objectification, and the Desire to Conform*, was an American Library Association Stonewall Honor Book. Her latest title, the novel *Sketchtasy*, was one of NPR's Best Books of 2018.

Sycamore's writing has appeared in a wide variety of publications, including the *San Francisco Chronicle*, *Bookforum*, *Boston Review*, BOMB, *The Baffler*, *Fence*, *Ploughshares*, *New Inquiry*, *Los Angeles Review of Books*, and more.

Sycamore's novels include *So Many Ways to Sleep Badly* and *Pulling Taffy*, and her anthologies include *Nobody Passes: Rejecting the Rules of Gender and Conformity* and *That's Revolting! Queer Strategies for Resisting Assimilation*. Her next anthology, *Between Certain Death and a Possible Future: Queer Writing on Growing up with the AIDS Crisis*, will be published by Arsenal Pulp Press in Fall 2021. Mattilda is currently working on *Touching the Art*, a book about her fraught relationship with her late grandmother, a visual artist from Baltimore. Sycamore lives in Seattle, where she loves the rain almost as much as she loves the sun.